HOW
INTO THE MOVIES -
AND HOW YOU
CAN TOO!

For Corinne—
Here's to happy endings!
Sincerely, Yoppel
Leona

HOW I BROKE INTO THE MOVIES - AND HOW YOU CAN TOO!

Tips, True Experiences
and Interesting
Insights Bring You the
Big Picture

Leona Weiss Toppel

CONTENTS

DEDICATION

For someone *extra* special from his special extra . . .

Throughout our marriage my husband Bert *always* has stood at my side encouraging me, lifting my spirits and helping me to cope when I've felt all "coped-out". When I started working in films, the strain on him was obvious. It was difficult for him not to worry when I drove off into the dark of morning to a less than prime location.

His kisses and hugs, which always greet me as I come through the door, and his pride when he sees me on the screen mean a lot and he knows that when I say "I love you for your support", I'm *not* acting

And here's a thank you to those stars who treat us extras with the respect and consideration that any human being deserves . . . even though we're "only atmosphere".

INTRODUCTION

I've driven a pace car in front of an automobile driven by Robert DiNiro. I've been hooked up to an IV in a Chicago hospital. I've been a hateful social worker. I've been a tough cigar smoking old crone. I've been a homeless person . . . several times. I've been an overly enthusiastic ringside spectator at an illegal boxing match. I've been a nun. I've been an attorney. I've been a screaming passenger in an airliner entreating God almighty to keep me safe. I've been held hostage by two mean automatic gun totting dudes who'd just as soon shoot ya as look at ya. I've spent two days in a roach infested women's prison (that bright orange jump suit just wasn't "me"). I've been a con artist. I've been a teacher. I've been high society. I've been low down. I've done the Florence Nightingale bit. I've been all of these and many more. All of the above mentioned adventures were make-believe, acting jobs in theatrical films, commercials, industrial films, and public service announcements. Since 1983, while working in films as an extra and as a principal, I've had more fun than a mouse in a brie factory. Working in the movies is an experience one savors-especially if one is the kind of gung-ho fan I am.

Although this book deals primarily with what it's like being an extra (aka background artist or atmosphere), I've included information about being a principal, because while being an extra can be lots of fun, getting even *one line* in a major motion picture can have you walking on cloud 27 (that's three times better than cloud nine). I know. It happened to me. And you know what? *You* have the potential to get involved in the business, too. These days the industry is looking for "real people" to be "reel people"—not the mannequins of long ago.

As you read about some of my experiences and the experiences of some of my movie friends, perhaps you'll discover that you may want to get involved in a business that has given me a great deal of pleasure, and a bit of pain—but only a bit. Of course, you may decide that a life of poverty isn't for you; this, after all, a democracy.

Even if you don't want to join the movie business work force, I think you'll have fun reading about what goes on behind the scenes. And the more you learn, the greater your next movie-going experience will be.

As far as I'm concerned, working on a shoot is like eating pizza: even one that's not perfect is better than none at all.

CHAPTER I

Sex And Debauchery or Now That I Have Your Attention, Here's How I Fell in Love with the Movies

Keep your Junior Mints, keep your gigantic buckets of popcorn, keep your super-sized, over-priced, over-iced soft drinks. For *me* sandwiches and the movies go together like Laurel and Hardy.

The earliest memory I have concerning the movies involves my coming home from school, being given a sandwich and going to the local movie house. I didn't go to the movies *every* day—only two or three times a week, although two or three times a *day* would have been more to my liking.

Every time I entered that glitzy theater, and in those days movie houses *were* glitzy, I was swept into a world that fired my imagination and made me want to be part of what was going on up on that screen. Of course, I knew there was no way that could happen. How could a little girl from a suburb of Chicago *ever* be in the movies?

Oak Park, Illinois was only 20 miles from Chicago, over 2,000 miles from Hollywood, but an impossible journey to the silver screen. I had no way of knowing that many years later the mountain would come to Mohammed. By Hollywood's coming to Chicago, I'd get the opportunity to be a small part of that crazy business. Would I *take* the opportunity? You betcha!

I don't remember ever going to the movies with my mother *and* father at the same time. They took turns going to "the show", as they called the movies, because they owned a mom-and-pop grocery/deli which was open seven days a week from seven in the morning until well past midnight. My folks' store was special: It was known throughout that affluent suburb as *the* place to get top-notch salads, Boston baked beans, roast beef, corned beef, baked ham (how could a Jewish couple—who never even *tasted* it make such a treat!), rye bread, oysters, gourmet, imported delicacies (pickled walnuts, rattlesnake meat, marinated watermelon rinds, etc.). *All* of the meats and salads were homemade, as were the Boston baked beans—which were a knockout, even people from Boston said so.

These gastronomic delights were prepared by my mother with considerable help from my older sister and my aunt. But most of the work fell on my mom's shoulders, even though she was ill enough to require surgery at least five times, that I can remember. Every morning at dawn, my dad would go to the area's finest bakery and pick up the breads and pastry. He made several trips—each time returning to the store with huge, heavy trays piled high.

My big brother didn't help much because in the 1930s and 1940s cooking was "women's work". Besides, he was the family genius who was graduated at the top of his class and attended the University of Chicago on a scholarship. Since he ended up as a high-ranking member of the State Department, which brought pleasure to the rest of the family, his contribution, while "different", was a contribution nevertheless.

An easy life it wasn't, even for me, the baby of the family. I did what I could: From age five, I waited on customers—which seemed to amuse them, except for the time I observed a patron whose makeup looked as if it had been applied by Dali. With glee I shouted, "Oh, look, Mama! A clowney!" I also delivered grocery orders; sometimes I had to travel as much as eight blocks. This was a time when supermarkets weren't around, when the "personal touch" was the norm—rather than the exception between the grocer and the customers. I would walk long distances clutching two huge brown bags, (good conditioning for carrying heavy wardrobe bags later in my life) reach my destination and sometimes receive a DIME TIP! Most of my spending money came from my meager allowance and from my retrieving coins which had been dropped during busy times in the store. The coins would sometimes roll under shelves and at the end of the day I'd seek them as diligently as a gold miner panning for nuggets.

My father named our store The Paradise Food Shop:one of the great misnomers of the century, although I suppose that for a young Russian immigrant who arrived to these shores with little more than his clothes and a few rubles, having his establishment in such a prestigous community must have *seemed* like paradise, The Oak Park venue was his second store (he sold the Chicago business in order to move his family to a community with better schools and with more economic opportunities). It was short of paradise for the rest of us–even though we knew that our dad was doing his best for us

There were no vacations with *both* my parents. While other families were frolicking on the beach and picnicking, our group ate dinner in shifts because a couple of us had to be available to wait on customers. We were so tired at the end of a busy Saturday or Sunday that we could barely drag ourselves to our flat in the next block. If that was paradise—then I'll take Peoria.

We lived in a flat above a jewelry store on a busy main street–the end of the line for the town's noisy streetcars. You can get used to most things. I say we *lived* in the flat, but in reality it served primarily as a place to sleep: Three bedrooms, a large living room, a good-sized dining room, a bathroom and a *huge* kitchen. But huge as the kitchen was, all the cooking was done in the back of the store. The flat *was* used for occasional family get-togethers. My dad loved paintings and statues and Louis the whatever furniture, oriental rugs and other ornate trappings. In other words, our apartment looked like an Antiques Roadshow gone haywire.

The back of the store—where we spent most of our waking hours— was furnished in early "The Honeymooners". The venue was augmented by a large round solid oak table and a tall secretary of cherry wood. Both these items were old, not in mint condition, but they'd be worth a small fortune today. Who knew? I also don't have my Shirley Temple doll, my decoder rings or my Little Big Books. There were several mismatched wooden chairs, a small sink, next to which was a range, a coal-burning furnace stood to the right of it and a well-worn velvet daybed was placed against the wall.. The back of the store had all the charm of a warehouse—which wasn't surprising since cases of canned goods were stored on high wooden shelves which ran the length of the room. There was a toilet. Oh, yes, the toilet. The toilet was housed in a room just a tad larger than a phone booth, but this phone booth also contained a rusty pail and a tired old string mop. No curtains, no ceramic tile, no matching rug and towels. Merely a commode inside a cramped, shabby space. The wooden door closed with a metal hook & eye. Although the back room was warm—and in a strange way cozy— during the winter months, in the summer the heat and the humidity were depressing—sometimes close to debilitating. Air conditioning wasn't a "given" in those days—unless one counts opening the back door as "air conditioning". With all that, it was still better than some of the holding areas I'd occupy years later.

Dinnertime was a study in cholesterol—typical of Old World cooking. The dinnertime motto was, "If it tastes good, it's good for you". *These* days, if it tastes good, it's not good for you! Food was important in our home (besides that which we sold in our store). Our ethnic cuisine wasn't only delicious, it was a bright spot in a tough day that often was made even tougher by the taunts of some of my classmates who believed that the Jews *did* kill Jesus—and it was my fault. Matter of fact, in those days, Oak Park was the kind of place that was best described by native son Ernest Hemingway as "the village of broad lawns and narrow minds".

So what does all of this have to do with my love of the movies? Plenty. I've yet to go to a shrink to get the official word on the workings of my mind, but I know that there were things about the movies that brought me into a world where moms *and* dads did stuff with their kids *together*: going on picnics, taking vacations, going to the beach, having dinner together in a real dining room. In the movies, America's curly-topped darling, Shirley Temple went from rags to riches in only ninety minutes while tippy-tapping her little heart out. In the movies, Andy Hardy's biggest worry was winning back the affections of his girlfriend Polly. For those of you who are too young to remember the Andy Hardy movies, see if you can rent one of them at the video shop. Look under the section titled "They don't make 'em like this anymore."

In the movies the kitchens were bright and cheery—and the bathrooms had cute curtains, rugs and sometimes a green plant! In the movies the furnace was in the *basement*, and kids did their homework in their bedrooms, rather than in the midst of crocks of Boston baked beans.

There was *more* to like about going to the movies: During those hot summer months, it was an oasis, a marble lobbied, crystal chandeliered palace resplendent with winding stairways, plush seats, balconies—and sometimes even twinkling "stars" in the ceiling. The silver and blue banner hanging from the marquee beckoned with "Air-cooled inside". What a joy it was to go from that stuffy store to a refreshing movie house showing me bits of lives fascinating, new and exciting.

My mother had her special reason for attending the movies: the free dishes that were given to each woman who presented a ticket on, as I recall, a Wednesday. So even the china on which I ate had a movie connection. Cream-colored, with a burgundy band outlined in gold—I was *sure* that Shirley Temple had those very same dishes on her dining table. Well, it wasn't *impossible*.

There were several occasions when I got my few moments of fame *in front* of the silver screen—if not *on* it. Between the Movietone News and the feature presentation I was accorded the honor of standing on the stage of the local movie house and selecting the numbers for the Screeno game (a kind of Bingo). Cash prizes were awarded, with yours truly receiving the magnificent sum of one dollar. It was always crisp. It was the best buck I ever clutched in my sweaty little hand. And boy, oh, boy did I dress up for the event! I remember an especially spiffy organdy number: It was light purple, highly starched and looked smashing with my black patent slippers and white socks. Topping off that picture of high fashion was a bow—but not just any bow. Catching the long curls at the side of my head was a bow the size of that dining room table. Even with half my peripheral vision obscured, I noticed how proud my relatives were. (Isn't it cute the way she puts her hand into the box and pulls out a piece of paper with a number on it?!"). And to think that I did that with no rehearsal. I realized at that moment that show business was in my blood. Actually, in his youth, my dad was an actor. So here was another ham in the family deli!

I can't remember ever having anything less than a good time at the movies—whether I was picking Screeno numbers, going to the show with my friends on a Saturday afternoon or having a date with my current one-and-only . . . forever, or for three weeks–whichever came first.

Now, years and years later, I'm actually involved in the making of films—and I've gotta tell you, it sure beats picking Screeno numbers. Each day working on a set is a potpourri of surprises, a cornucopia of experiences. I only wish I had started in the movie business at the same time my folks had me working in the grocery store.

I'm often asked by young adults if they should take the plunge into the pool of talent out there. It's a huge pool–more like an ocean, actually. There are undercurrents, gigantic waves and a myriad of strange creatures floating around. If you think those waves in a "Perfect Storm" were overwhelming, just try keeping afloat in show business. In spite of all those potential problems, I tell them to jump in while they're young, because if they never try, they'll spend the rest of their lives wondering "what if?" Someone said, "It's better to *try something* and fail then to *try nothing* and succeed." How true.

CHAPTER II

How Would You Like To Be a Mother?

The Day Fate Became My Agent

Fast forward to my adult years. I had been writing for a Chicago newspaper—which got plenty for its money: I did restaurant reviews, theater reviews, interviews with business, industry and show business personalities in addition to a commentary type of column, which enabled me to spill my guts about a variety of subjects. I enjoyed writing all the columns—but as it turned out two of the columns were responsible for my finding a new career. To be accurate, the *career* found me . . . in a way that amazes me still. The combination of one of my theater review columns and one of my interviews brought me into the world of motion pictures.

A comedy came into town. I reviewed it, and although "Sheer Madness" wasn't much more than a bit of amusing fluff, it was an entertaining evening in the theater. As it turned out, I was just about the only reviewer who wrote favorably about it. The co-producers were so pleased that they sent me a note expressing their appreciation. "Sheer Madness" played Chicago for over 15 years until it lost its home.

Shortly after the "Sheer Madness" opening, I interviewed a filmmaker by the name of Jack Sell. He had won a couple of awards for his industrial films, his political bits or one or another of his pieces.

I didn't see or hear from the "Sheer Madness" people again until I got an invitation from co-producers Bruce Jordan and Marilyn Abrams. They were celebrating an anniversary of their production in Chicago.

The cocktail party was to be held in a tony high-rise overlooking Lake Michigan.

When I arrived, whom should I see but Jack Sell. He was wearing a long black cape which made him look a lot like Mandrake the Magician. I had no way of knowing that Sell, like a magician, would one day do a disappearing act of his own. After the usual obligatory cocktail chatter, Sell told me that he had recently finished a screenplay that he also was going to direct and produce. He said I'd be great as the mother in the film. You'd think that at my age I would have had enough sense to have asked him what the movie was about. But the old Ms. Ego took over and I agreed to do my first film for this person who gave the impression of being a clean-cut, ethical prince of a fellow.

The deal was this: I'd play the part of The Mother. I'd be paid $250 . . . *if* he made money on the film. The other actors and actresses had the same kind of deal—or so I was told. I had several lines in Sell's "epic" (most of which I was asked to improvise), in addition to some background work. I also worked in a commercial for it. To call the movie a disaster would be much too generous; I didn't know what I was getting into. During the first day of shooting, dinner consisted of warm Pepsi and cold pizza consumed in an alley next to the Chicago Theater off State Street in the heart of the Loop. Everything about the production shrieked CHEAP! But what did I know? I was in a movie for the first time.

Between takes, after that sumptuous repast, I remarked to a young actor seated next to me, "Isn't this great? This is so much fun!" The fellow looked at me the way one might look at an individual of diminished capacity and replied, "This sucks! If you want to work in a *decent* movie, I'll give you the name of one of my agents. Sign up with her, she'll get you work". I did just that—and the following week, I was performing in a television movie as an extra. That's how it started.

As for that first movie, "Outtakes" turned out to be an R-rated flick, the "R" must have stood for repulsive, with no socially redeeming aspects. What is was was just plain dirty. It wasn't clever, it wasn't funny. The primary rule of blue comedy is that it's got to be funny—or else it's going to be only dirty—and only dirty is, quite frankly, a bore.

To give you some idea of the quality of this piece of garbage, here's how one of my scenes went: I'm in my daughter's new apartment. She's doing the dishes in her little kitchen. I'm sipping tea in the adjacent living room while complimenting her good taste. The phone rings. I was supposed to answer it and then improvise. No one told me that the phone on the table behind me was in the shape of a male organ—and I don't mean a kidney. The phone rings, my daughter asks me to answer it. I turn, I see the appendage-shaped phone and I improvise, "If you think I'm going to reach out and touch *that*, you're very much mistaken". With no modesty, I'll tell you that that was one of the film's better moments. You can imagine how lame the rest of the script was.

"Outtakes" played for one week at a small theater in Chicago. Jack Sell moved to California without paying the actors. I found out that he was ensconced in an office on Los Angeles' posh Wilshire Blvd. On vacation one summer, I went up there and guess what! He wasn't there— or so his receptionist said. I left him a note—something less than a Valentine. Since that time, I understand that he sold the movie to some overseas outfit. Several fellow actors took the movie out of a video store. Will this indignity ever end? Did Sell make any money on his first theatrical effort? I don't know. I *do* know that, thankfully, my movie career has been moving upward since. It *had* to.

CHAPTER III

A "TYPICAL DAY" ON THE SET?

FUHGEDABOUDIT!

How do I write about a "typical day" on the set, when there's no such thing? Actually, that's just *one* of the things I love about being in the movie business. I never know when I get the call from my agent what the day will bring.

Of course, I know where I'm going, an automobile is usually a "must", I know what wardrobe to bring, it's usually wear one outfit, bring three outfits—unless the film is a period piece—and then even the extras are dressed by wardrobe. For women the period makeup is applied and they are professionally coiffed. Men must have haircuts of the period. I also know,, of course, what time I'm to be on the set. Once or twice I had a 5:30 A.M. call, but usually the call is 7 or 8. I never know what time we'll wrap and I don't ask, 'cause no one knows and no one appreciates the question. Working in the movies isn't like working in an office from nine to five, five days a week. Sometimes we work all night (from five or six in the evening until seven or eight the next morning). Sometimes there is a Sunday shoot and sometimes a Saturday shoot.

Here's as close to a "typical day" as I can paint for you. It all starts when I get a call from my agent; the call can come anywhere from a day before to several days before the shoot. On one occasion, I got a call at midnight for a 7 A.M. call, but that hardly ever happens, so don't sweat it. The initial call from my agent asks if I'm available. If I am, I'm told to call back the next day for place, time and wardrobe requirements.

Why am I not told right then? Because the agent doesn't know. No one knows what will be needed the next day and at what time until the end of that day's shoot. So I call back when I'm told, put together my wardrobe in a clothing bag, check out the car (enough gas? tires O.K.? etc.). I try to get a good night's sleep although the night before a shoot—either as an extra or as a principal—sleep seems to come in fifteen minute bits. The next morning I dress in one of the outfits I was told to bring. I select the most comfortable, and I'm out of the door 45 minutes earlier than the trip requires—more if the weather is bad. Shoots don't get canceled because of a little (or a lot) of ice and snow, and in the movie business, being on time isn't just desired, it's required. The phrase "time is money" probably originated on the set of some film.

Upon arriving at the location I park my car. The production company pays parking fees—but you're on your own if you use public transportation. Don't ask me *why*—I just work here. Depending upon how far the parking lot is from the holding area, I either walk or am shuttled. Generally, if the distance is more than three blocks from the parking lot/holding area, shuttle service is provided.

The first thing I do upon entering the holding area is find a place to hang my wardrobe. No place to hang my stuff?—Well, there's always the floor or a chair—unless they're all needed for seating. One of the things I like about period pieces is that, because the wardrobe is supplied, there's no lugging a wardrobe from home and back again—a wardrobe that may not even be utilized.

Checking in with the coordinator comes next. The coordinator usually is an individual from my agent's office, who keeps track of all the extras and sends the required background to the set on request of the a.d. (assistant director—or one of his or her assistants). It's the coordinator who also checks me *out*—but not until *much* later.

As I look around the room, I usually see people I know 'cause I've been around a long time. But even if I'm the only "old timer", I can sit with anyone and feel welcome. By virtue of the fact that we're all in that room we've got the beginning of a beautiful friendship. If the production company has any heart at all, we'll get coffee and sweet rolls, which we devour with the enthusiasm of seven year locusts. The considerate extra takes just one roll until everyone has a chance to get a sugar rush.

Our feeding frenzy is interrupted by the appearance of the people from wardrobe who either: O.K. what we're wearing, O.K. *part* of what we're wearing and have us make changes from our own wardrobe or send us to the wardrobe trailer for a complete or partial overhaul. While waiting to be called to the set, I sign my voucher, a piece of paper that, after it's filled out with my name, address, phone number, social security number, time in, etc., will serve as proof of my presence on the set. At the end of the day the coordinator will fill in the wrap time, sign it and give me a copy for my records.

This particular scene is an exterior for the film "Miracle on 34th Street". The temperature is hovering at 80 degrees and we extras must look as if we're on the brink of turning into Popsicles. On go our coats, boots, hats, earmuffs, gloves, scarves—and all those other pieces of wearing apparel that are dandy for a trek to the Arctic, but are murder when most sane people are at the beach or, better yet, ensconced in an air conditioned apartment. We're herded to a parking lot (we'll be working in front of a green screen) where we're told to "look cold" as we're waiting for news of Santa's trial. I'm placed in front of the camera, bundled up to my nose. I do a subtle version of the "Winter-in-Chicago-Hop" while blowing into my cupped hands. "That's great!", says the director. Do it that same way on the next take". Between takes we remove our coats, and are given small paper cups of water . . . so that we don't faint—and hold up production. This goes on for a couple of hours after which we're sent back to the holding area where some cookies have been left for us. We eat them. Extras eat whatever and whenever they can. They also go to the bathroom whenever the opportunity arises because we never know when the chance will come our way again.

In a couple of hours we're sent out again and moved around so that the group that was in front is now in the back. A couple more hours of pretty much the same kind of torture and we're back in the holding area where we have our lunch, sit around for several of hours and then comes the call. "It's a wrap!". With that call of freedom we descend upon the check-out table to have our vouchers signed before we pile into the vans that will take us back to the parking facility. From the time I left my house that day until I pull into my garage, some 12 hours have passed.

I've told you about one of the less exciting days in the life of an extra because if you still want to be an extra after a day like *that*, then *you're* the kind of person who's going to make one heck of a good one. You're going to survive working in bitter cold. You're going to work in driving snow and wind with your head held high. You're not going to feel "hurt" if you're left sitting in the holding area as one of a few extras who weren't selected for a given scene. You're *never* going to ask, "when can I go home?", even as your working day is going into the 12th hour. You're going to follow *all* the rules as a good sport should. And you're going to do all this for the usual fee of $55.00 for eight hours plus time and a half for overtime *minus* 10 percent for your agent . . . minus all kinds of taxes. If you drive, there's gas and toll expenses. Not much left after all the subtracting.

Because there is no such thing as a "typical day" on the set, if day one is lousy for you, day two may be great. You just don't know. Being an extra is for the person who likes adventure, who knows how to take orders—*fast*, who can get along with all kinds of people, who is independent. 'Fraidy cats need not apply.

Now that I've told you about one of my less stimulating acting days, I'm going to share with you just a few of those experiences which had me saying to myself, "I can't believe I'm getting paid for doing this", little as that pay may be!

So read on, my dears, and find out what *this* actress has been doing all these years, because my experiences may be a lot like what could happen to you should you decide to go down the yellow brick road to the land of Oz. Warning! Watch out for those mean "witches" along the way.

CHAPTER IV

I Was Told to Pat
Paul Newman on the Shoulder:

Little Pleasures, Big Breaks . . . and Bad Hair Days

If the pay stinks—which it does, if extras are often treated like dirt—which they are, if the working conditions can be a nightmare—why would anyone with an IQ even ten points higher than a turnip want to be part of this movie-making business? Why? Because most of us love being even a tiny part of that gigantic undertaking. Of course, we're hoping that one day we'll get a speaking role . . . if only one sentence, which means considerably more money.

We love working in the same scene with big stars. We love being on the "inside" when so many people would give their eye teeth to do what we do for nothing, which is just about what we get. I can't tell you how many times that spectators—known as "civilians" try to sneak into a scene thinking no one will notice them. We do. We love seeing how truly great talents work. And, yes, we love seeing ourselves up there on the screen bigger than life—if only for a second. I know that no matter what happens to me, I'll be somewhere on films for many years to come.

The memories I have make it all worthwhile. Not all my memories are pleasant, but even the events that, at the time, seemed disastrous, now bring a smile to my lips.

Often a bit of the child comes out during our work. For an extra known among us as Bob the Troublemaker (as distinguished from Big

Bob—who wasn't a trouble maker) acting like a kid was what made Bob the lovable nut that he was. Bob was a firefighter who was an extra whenever his days off and the opportunity to work in a film jibed. The opportunity to play practical jokes on the rest of us seemed to be what he lived for. Bob's specialty was breaking up his fellow actors. My turn came during the filming of a real dog of a TV series called "Lady Blue".

The coordinator on the job was a woman whose unpleasant personality got on all our collective nerves. Truth to tell she was so ill-tempered, we were sure she was registered with the American Kennel Club. Because she was particularly nasty on that day, we all were ready for a laugh. But why then and why me?

The scene we were shooting took place in an office. Bob the Troublemaker was sitting at his desk. I was standing near him pretending to be asking him a question about a letter I was holding (no lines, just miming). About two minutes into the scene, a detective, gun drawn, burst into the office and shouted to one of the fellows at another desk, "You're under arrest for laundering money—and that's just for starters!" Well, actually, those last two words came out "Fa statas", because the actor playing the part of the detective had a New York accent. As the scene was being rehearsed, Bob whispered to me in a voice *just* loud enough for me and me alone to hear, "Fa statas? Fa statas? What are fa statas?" I begged, "Please, Bob, knock it off." Bob showed no mercy. Then, just as the cameras were about to roll for the take, Bob whispered in the tiniest voice I've ever heard come from a grown male, "I know! Fa statas are what you order in a Mexican restaurant. Waiter! Bring me a platter of fa statas!" With that I could no longer contain that pent-up blast of laughter that finally made it's way out of my innards, past my lips with one of those disgusting piggy sounds that pierced the "seriousness" of the scene.

Everything came to a halt. "Cut! Do you *mind*?! We're trying to film here!" I was embarrassed beyond turning red. I was told I was into sheet-white. Why I wasn't thrown off the set, I don't know. And what of Bob? Good old Bob sat at his desk looking as surprised as everyone else at my unprofessional behavior. Bob sat there looking like a cherub. I *think* I saw a halo around his head.

Some day I'm going to get back at you, Bob. You can count on it. I don't see you these days because you took some kind of test and you were promoted to fire captain. But like I said, I'll get you—so watch your back.

As I noted before, most of the time we extras are instructed to bring three or four changes to each job, but for the film "She's Having a Baby" we didn't have to bother taking all those clothes with us because we had to wear the same outfit for six days straight. Had the scene required casual clothes, the problem, which lasted for almost a week, wouldn't have arisen. Casual clothes usually are washable, so even if one is dog-tired after work one could throw a few things into a washing machine and then feel band-box fresh for the next day's shoot. Not so when one is wearing dressy duds that require dry cleaning only.

The scene I worked in took place in a church where the principals were being wed. As the wedding guests, we extras had to sit in our pews for six days, although we *did* get to go home to our loved ones each evening. During the scene we *all* spoke: we recited the "Our Father" at least 30 times. No, we didn't get paid extra for speaking. There is a rule called the omni. If the extra speaks during a scene, there's additional money provided there are four or less in the scene. Five or more—no extra money. Sometimes extras are told to shout in a scene and then when the film is released, stock sound is dubbed in. I suspect that this is done so that we extras don't get to make a few additional dollars. I wish I could be that sure about next week's lottery numbers. With all the money that's wasted during the making of a movie, it makes us extras wonder why the production companies are so chintzy when it comes to giving us an extra sweet roll or a sandwich or, best of all, *more money*. We're always being told how important we are to the production by the a.d.'s—or on occasion, even by the director—but most of the time we know those are just words said to keep our energy up during a long day of shooting.

The fact of the matter is that we *are* important. Picture this: It's a gigantic Biblical production. Moses reaches the Red Sea, it parts, he starts to cross, but no one is following him to the Promised Land.

No one. Not a man, not a woman, not a child, not one person. Pretty dull.

Picture this: General Sherman is marching through Atlanta—solo. Exciting, realistic? I don't think so

Picture this: Cleopatra is reclining on her barge, but she's going nowhere. She's just dead in the waters of the Nile because there are no extras to paddle her canoe. You get the idea.

Extras give a film the realistic quality it requires. So why don't we get more money? Supply and demand. There are literally *thousands* of extras in the Chicagoland area alone—all vying for *many* fewer part.

When extras are asked to bring their cars to a shoot they earn an additional $15.00-$20.00 (whoop-de-doo!). My 1977 Chevy had been in several films, but a couple occasions stand out.

In the film "Midnight Run", I was to drive a pace car in front of an automobile driven by Robert Di Niro in which Charles Grodin was a passenger. "Lee", explained the a.d., "I want you to drive at a speed that will keep them just this far from you." He spread his arms to give me some idea of the distance the scene required. And then he added, "They're going to be right behind you as you're racing down the street. At one point *they're* going to turn off to the right, but you just keep going straight. Don't stop. There will be a p.a. down the street to flag you down and then you drive back here." Sounded simple enough.

The only "nerves" I had was sitting in my car, looking into my rear-view mirror and seeing Di Niro and Grodin sitting there. What if I did something wrong during the take . . . like losing control of the car? After the a.d. called "Action", and I started driving, I felt more relaxed. The Di Niro car turned off to the right, I kept going—and started looking for that p.a.. Nothing. I kept looking. No p.a.. About two miles later I found myself following a tow truck in the middle of the Loop! Being the bright woman that I am, I decided that something had gone wrong, and perhaps I'd better take it upon myself to get back to where I started.

When I got back, there was the a.d. who told me how sorry he was that he forgot to put a p.a. out on the street to flag me down. This was one time I didn't do exactly as I was told. Good thing—or I might *still* be driving straight ahead.

Another driving experience involved not just my car and one other, but several dozen cars. Before lunch, between scenes on the film "Running Scared", the head stunt man announced that he wanted to meet with all the extras who were told to bring their cars. He wanted to see us after the meal, and I can tell you that the talk among us at lunch wasn't about the weather. When the head stunt person wants to have a meeting with you, you can be darn sure that you're going to be asked to do more than drive around the block.

For this scene, at O'Hare Airport, we were to be driving down the highway. No big deal. But the après lunch get-together gave us additional news about what would be going on during the shoot. The stunt coordinator explained that we'd be placed, one car behind the other, on both sides of the road and at his signal we'd flow into formation. We were told to drive 35 miles an hour leaving a given amount of space behind, in front of, and on either side of the cars around us. This information, while a *bit* more complex than merely driving down the highway, still didn't raise our blood pressures more than a couple of points.

What made us a tad concerned was when the stunt coordinator said, "Don't change anything you're doing, no matter what's happening. A couple of cars may zoom in front of you, but don't worry about it. You just follow instructions and no one will get hurt." And no one will get hurt?! Those last few words made me feel as if I were in the middle of a stagecoach robbery. We all followed instructions—and *that* time I didn't end up in the middle of the Loop behind a tow truck.

One of the things to remember when you're an extra or a principal is this: Never say you can't do something—*unless* doing said thing will cause you or some other decent citizen great bodily harm. Point in fact: A pub scene in the film "Only the Lonely". I was sitting at a table with my "date", whose real name was Reno [his mother liked the biggest little city in Nevada—thus his name. It could have been worse. What if she was nuts about Las Vegas?] Anyway, we were placed right behind the movie's star John Candy. The a.d. approached us and explained he wanted to see lots of smoke arising from our table. "You smoke, don't you?", he asked Reno. Reno said that, although he used to smoke, after his heart surgery he gave up the habit. "You smoke, don't you, Lee?" "Of course", I answered, which wasn't *exactly* a fib. When I was a sophomore in high school I smoked my *first* cigarette (not a funny one) in the ladies room of a local movie house. It also was my *last* cigarette. But, hey, if I had said "no", Reno and I would have been relegated to some obscure space on the set.

So there I was with a full pack of cigarettes–the kind that that cowboy smokes on his way to his last roundup. "O.K., Lee," said the a.d., "let's see lots of smoke!" With that, he left. I started smoking. I started smoking the way a non-smoker smokes—much to the delight of Reno, whose back, thankfully was to the camera. The more *I* puffed, the greener I became and the redder *Reno* became from trying to suppress a laugh. Since I was put on the Earth to spread happiness, I fluttered my lashes just the tiniest bit, which caused Reno to practically go into a mini—seizure. Fearing for his well-being, I confined my actions to puffing and blowing.

My personal homage to the Chicago Fire resulted in enough smoke to process a ton of kippers. I did a sterling job. So what if I *did* get so sick to my stomach that I had all I could do to keep from tossing my cookies? What happened? The scene ended up on the cutting room floor. But not to worry. A scene that Reno and I had involving two elderly gentlemen carrying a deceased friend into the pub for a farewell nightcap showed us for a good, three seconds—which is great camera time for an extra.

The movie "End of the Line" (a bit of artistic cinema art which reached the end of the line much sooner than the producers would have wished) starred Wilford Brimley with a small part played by Rita Jenrette When wardrobe saw my suit—they *loved* it. Perfect. Two hours later, I was told to change into a different outfit because Ms. Jenrette was wearing a suit of the exact color. The fact that *I* had mine on *first* held no water—don't be ridiculous.

A lawyer and her client. In case you're confused,
I'm the one on the left. Kidding around at "Lady Blue"

Later that day in my other outfit I was standing next to Brimley during
a lull while the lights were being adjusted. Knowing that extras weren't
supposed to speak to a principal unless the principal spoke to them
first, I noticed that Brimley smiled at me—and—when you come to
think of it—a smile is *almost* like saying "hello". So very softly I said to
him, "I really admire your work". "WHAT DID YOU SAY?" boomed
Brimley. Boy, oh, boy was *I* in trouble. I had no choice but to repeat
my statement. "I said, I really admire your work". To which he replied,
"OH, I HEARD YOU THE *FIRST* TIME! I JUST LOVE IT WHEN
PEOPLE TELL ME THAT! " Whatta nice guy.

Working with children really is work! I'm no W.C. Fields when it
comes to my feelings for the little rug-wetters, but children tend to be
their own directors. Kids don't want to wait for the lighting to be moved,
or for the sound to be adjusted. Kids want to do their thing when the
Muse beckons. The younger the child, the less time he/she has for
"fooling around" with lighting, camera angles and all the other stuff.

During the filming of an episode of "Missing Persons", I played a
nanny in a day care center. Among the youngsters were an adorable three-

year-old who had sparkling brown eyes and a smile that could melt hearts, a four-year-old flaxen-haired girl who had the look of a haughty 45-year-old society matron, another three-year-old, who knew how to speak and understood what we were saying—but chose not to, and ANTHONY. ANTHONY was the size of Montana—which would have been O.K., if he had been a friendly state. The child looked like a Sumo wrestler on steroids. Some of my best friends are Sumo wrestlers. But, ANTHONY wasn't friendly; ANTHONY was obnoxious, uncontrollable, destructive, stubborn—and silent. ANTHONY reminded me of a science fiction robot who rampages through New York City and leaves nothing standing. Several adults were unable to reason with him. But then I've never seen anyone try to reason with Godzilla either. ANTHONY was eventually removed from the set and returned to his mother, who was just barely five feet and weighed, I'll bet, no more than a hundred pounds. She seemed to be a bit higher up on the food chain than her son.

The child who was in my charge for the scene was the three-year-old with the sparkling brown eyes. Nicholas was angelic, he seemed to be in awe of all the lights and the other paraphernalia required to produce a television film. Nicholas didn't opt to walk with me. He seemed to like me well enough, it was just that, unlike ANTHONY, he didn't care to move—which he was supposed to do. Finally, I picked him up and whispered softly in his ear, "Nicholas, you are the *best* boy in this entire building. And you know what? I think Santa is going to bring you lots of toys for Christmas. Christmas will be here very soon. Santa sure likes good boys!"

I made this my mantra for Nick, which I repeated for the entire scene. The director *loved* my "pick-him-up-and-whisper" m.o. Nicholas' mother was not as enthusiastic about my toy promises—but I'm sure she was thrilled when she saw her pride and joy on television about a month later. Perhaps, someday, somewhere ANTHONY will get another opportunity to grace a movie or TV screen or perhaps, when he gets older, he'll opt to be a teamster.

My experience with two other boys during the filming of another television series was quite different—and bittersweet. It was Cuba in the 1930s. Make that Lake Bluff in 1993. In this episode of "The Untouchables" a Lake Bluff mansion "played the part" of a Cuban orphanage.

I was one of the nuns charged with taking care of the youngsters.

My responsibility for the scene on that particular day was to transport a boy via wheelchair. Ordinarily this wouldn't have created a problem. But there were a few extenuating circumstances: The youngster was afflicted with multiple sclerosis—which again, wouldn't have been a problem if the 1930s wheelchair hadn't been made out of oak and wicker; the production company was meticulous about keeping everything authentic. The wheelchair in which the child arrived was a '90s, modern, state-of-the-art piece of equipment that supported his head. They tried padding, they tried blankets, they tried whatever they could as support for his head and shoulders. Nothing worked: The child simply didn't have the muscle tone to sit upright.

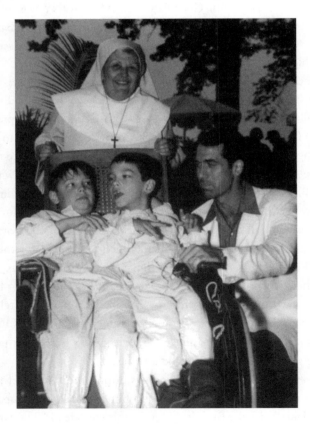

Here I am as a Cuban nun with my charges
and Ness in the television series "The Untouchables"

What to do? It was decided to put a second slender boy in the same wheelchair. Boy number two would put his arm around boy number one; a couple of buddies. It worked; they were a perfect pairing. The scene was ready to shoot. Whenever I'm an extra I decide what my "attitude" will be—relative to what's going on in the scene. Remember, I'm not allowed to speak, so I want to convey what I can through my actions just so they're not over the top. If the a.d. doesn't complain about it after the first take, I keep doing it take after take after take the same way. If the a.d. doesn't like what I'm doing, he/she will let me know. Once-in-a-while an a.d. will give me a "thumbs up".

During this segment, I decided I wanted to be a jolly nun—and I wanted my wheelchair passengers to be happy, as well. So I told the boys something I thought would make them laugh—and I told them the same thing at the same moment—to be sure that the continuity wasn't upset. It worked! The entire thing lasted less than a minute, but to this day it is one of my favorite scenes.

What made that moment especially memorable: The youngster with m.s. was in the scene because his mother had written to the Make-A-Wish Foundation. More than anything else the boy wanted to be on television. He got his heart's desire, and in doing so he won the hearts of all of us.

As I've mentioned, an actor never says "no" to a role, unless great bodily harm may be involved. So when my agent called and asked if I had a nun's costume for the film "Blue Chips" I answered, "I can get one!". "By tomorrow morning?" "No problem!". There *was* a problem: Within five minutes of that call I was phoning every convent within a ten mile radius. Everyone was very nice, but for various reasons, not one nun's habit was available.

I wondered why I was asked to bring my own costume. After all, this wasn't a shoe-string production by some fly-by-night operation. This was a film with Nick Nolte. "Blue Chips" was being shot in Chicago with my scene being shot at a Catholic school, in the gym where I was to be cheering my basketball team on to victory. BUT I NEEDED A NUN'S HABIT! I remembered seeing a shop in the local mall that just might solve my problem. I knew that they sold fright wigs. obnoxious masks that would scare the bejeabers out of Freddie Krueger, pretend doggie doo-doo, a potpourri of other equally tasteless knick knacks *and* some costumes. We're talking high class here. Lucky me. They had *one* nun's costume left. It was about $20.00 more than I wanted to spend (price tag: $23.00), but I was in a bind—so I put it on my charge card. Of course, for $23.00, I was looking at a habit that in no way could fool The Pope—or even an altar boy . . . *maybe* an Orthodox rabbi might be fooled—but not for long.

After I ironed the outfit, borrowed a large silver cross and a rosary from my neighbor, I looked pretty good. Besides, even cheapo outfits look better on film than they do in "real life". Off I went: A bargain basement Mother Theresa behind the wheel of a '77 Chevy. Perhaps it was my nun persona, but during the entire trip on the toll way to the location, not one car cut me off, not one driver gave me the single digit salute because I was traveling within the speed limit.

I arrived at the location to be greeted by the coordinator—who loved my outfit. She expressed the wish that the other extra would come dressed in the same kind of habit "So you could be from the same order." Same order? What same order? Our Lady of Trick or Treat? My sister colleague arrived several minutes after I and lo and behold, she also was wearing that same creation. Great, right? Wrong. When the head wardrobe person came around to look at us he exclaimed, with no small amount of disdain, "Nuns don't dress like that these days! They wear suits or jumpers with a headpiece." That was exactly what I had at home. While I was knocking myself out looking for a nun's costume, a perfectly suitable gray suit and cream-colored blouse were hanging in my closet. Within minutes off went my $23.00 investment and on went a grey jumper, cream-colored blouse and head covering. Twenty-three dollars down the drain! I was thinking thoughts no honest-to-goodness nun would ever entertain. What an awful start to the day. Things just *had* to get better. They did.

I was placed on a curved balcony overlooking the playing floor of the gym where the basketball game was to be taking place. To my left was an actor friend who was dressed as a priest. To his left stood Nick Nolte. To my right stood several others, including honest-to-goodness sports personalities, and additional extras. The game started and as I rooted for my team I put my palms together heaven-ward and once-in-awhile I'd cross myself (like right before a free-throw). My "priest" friend told me that Nolte got a kick out of my actions, and after the first take it seemed that Director William Friedkin did too. He ran over to me and exclaimed, "That was great! Do it the same way again on the next take!" I did.

After the movie was wrapped for the day, Director Friedkin came over to me, gave me a hug, a peck on the cheek and said, "You did a *great* job!" Carole, another nun/actress saw this, as did the other actors around us, and squealed, "Did you see that? Friedkin kissed Leona!" It's been a several years since that happened and each time we're together on a shoot, Carole tells everyone in earshot about that experience. I don't mind a bit.

I tell you this because hardly ever does a director come up to an actor and single him/her out for praise. I tell you this too, because this is an example of a seldom win-win situation. If Mr. Friedkin thought I was a *real* nun, then it meant that I did one heck of an Oscar-winning performance. If Friedkin thought I was "just background", and he was so pleased with my efforts, that he singled me out, I was still ahead of the game. To this day, I don't know if he thought I was a nun acting or an actress acting like a nun. Either way I was one happy extra that day.

Most of my extra friends love being in the ballroom scenes. They enjoy high profile cocktail party scenes, where they can wear their best gowns, jewels and furs. Please, no calls or letters from animal rights activists—I only work here. They also get a kick out of playing Chicago Gold Coast types shopping on Michigan Avenue or dining with the ritzy lunch bunch. Give me a wrinkled dress (which I keep rolled up in a bag between jobs), a pair of beat-up sneakers, a knit over-the-ears-hat and a pair of roll down hose. The part of a luckless old gal suits me just fine. I don't have to wear makeup—unless you consider having theatrical "dirt" smeared on my face and hands "makeup". I don't have to bring a change of wardrobe. I don't have to worry about spilling something on my costume during lunch. Best of all, I have the satisfaction of knowing that I *can* look better.

One day, dressed as above, I was sitting in Chicago's Union Station's main waiting room between takes when someone dropped a quarter in my lap. And I didn't have to give 10% of it to my agent.

In an independent film called "Ten Million Dollars and No Sense", I did a cameo as a tough, cigar chomping crone with heavy makeup, bad hair and a voice that any self-respecting Hell's Angel would be proud to have. I've been a mean, bigoted social worker ("Love Your Mama") with red tape where her heart should have been. No society matron she. Sometimes it feels good to be bad.

In "Time served" I was one tough inmate

"Tomorrow you'll be a biddy in "A League of Their Own", said my agent. Lucky me! Another glamour role! A *1940s* biddy was something new for me. I expected to have fun on the shoot—even though I wasn't

told what my biddy character would be doing in the scene. Upon arriving at the location for my 8:00 A.M. call, I checked in, giving my
name and the part I was to play. "Hi! I'm Leona Toppel; I'm the biddy."
"Fine, Leona, get over to wardrobe and after you get your stuff you'll
be shown to your trailer where you can get ready." *MY TRAILER!?* MY
GOODNESS! Generally, as far as I knew, only actors with lines got a
trailer! As I was changing into my 1940s duds (including stockings and
garters, not pantyhose), I marveled over my good fortune.. There I was
in that great trailer which contained a living room, kitchen and bathroom with shower. It sure beat getting dressed in a big common room
with all the other women extras.

Soon there was a knock on the door. A p.a. wanted to know what
I'd like for breakfast. Getting into the rhythm of life in a trailer, I
ordered orange juice (strained, please), lox and bagels, skimmed milk
and coffee cake. Just a simple meal. I didn't want to take advantage of
a good thing. I didn't have to worry. There wasn't going to be any
orange juice (strained *or* with pulp). No lox, no bagels, no milk, no
coffee cake, *and* no trailer. As it turned out, there was a mistake. I
was one of *four* biddies. There were to be three minor biddies and a
main biddy—who was late flying in from New York City. *THAT
TRAILER WAS FOR THE MAIN BIDDY.*

So much for my moment of feeling like a *star*. Actually, I was
beginning to feel more like a *nightlight* as I gathered up my stuff and
went off to change with the "common folks". What really "got me" was
why they had to fly in a main biddy from NYC. Chicago has biddies
up the gazoo. Another cinema mystery. By then it was evident that
"biddydom" was not my ticket to stardom.

After a terrific lunch (most of the dinners and lunches on location are
anywhere from good to if-there-were-a-restaurant-in-my-town-with-food-
this-good-I'd-eat-there-as-often-as-my-budget-would-allow) I sat around
shooting the breeze with the other two biddies and assorted other 1940s
characters. About nine hours passed and *finally* we were called to the set
where we were to sit in a three-biddy-line behind the MAIN BIDDY who
was in a radio studio expounding upon the evils of women playing baseball. I was the middle biddy, a sour pickle if there ever was one—and

proud of it. Ours was the last scene of the day. We wrapped at 7:00 P.M.—
and the director, Penny Marshall, gave each of us a long-stemmed white
rose. She sure knows how to make a movie . . . and how to say "thank you"
to three "minor biddies".

The production company of "Rookie of the Year" could have taken
lessons in employee relations from Ms. Marshall. The scenes that were
shot in Wrigley Field required hundreds of extras. Some "civilians"
were delighted to be involved just to be in a movie—even though
they'd be lost in the crowd. For those of us who were working for love
and money, we agreed that it was one of the two worst films (as far as
conditions were concerned) that we had ever worked on.

It was one of those shoots that was summer in the script, but fall in
reality. Just as trying to appear cold in hot weather is difficult, so is
trying to appear warm in cool weather. The hours were long and the
cheering we were required to do got to be a drag by the time half the
day was over. *AND* this was the straw that broke the extra's back . . .
OUR MEAL WASN'T SUPPLIED! We were expected to forage among
the fast food joints around the ball park.

Lest you think that we extras make too big a deal about the
meals and snacks served on a set, know that "feeding time" *is* a big
deal. When working on a film we're reminded to "keep up the
energy!" Food helps. Mealtime is also a welcome social break.
Strange as it may seem, what we extras are served often is a reflection
(at least to us) of the regard in which we're held. Too sensitive? Perhaps,
but how would you feel if you were served some so-so pasta while at
another table the cast, crew and even the security, who were hired to
control the traffic and gawkers, were shoveling in steak and crab legs?
Good meals and poor meals certainly fit into the "big breaks and bad
hair days" category for us extras.

"First the stars eat, then the cast and crew eat, then the flies eat,
then the extras eat". So goes a gag saying. Speaking of "gagging", the
all-time Slop Award goes to the food (and I use the term lightly) served
during the filming of "Gladiator" (not *that* one). How to describe it?
The word "glutinous" comes to mind.

One day we were served a yellow glutinous substance. A red glutinous substance was served the next day. Still another "meal" consisted of a layered glutinous combo. For us extras, the term "Run for the boarder" took on new meaning. But there *was* nowhere to run. We were a captive audience. We also received an apple *or* orange and a small pack of cookies (the highlight of the menu). As I stood in line with some 500 others, I felt a lot like Oliver Twist . . . without the "warm ambiance" that was enjoyed by that lad.

I have no way of knowing what the principals ate, but I'd be willing to bet my next residual check that "glutinous" was nowhere on the menu.

Generally, extras have much more modest meals than do the cast and crew although usually the food is good and plentiful: A choice of at least two entrees, vegetables, several salads and soft drinks, one or two desserts. Not bad. For some of the young, trying-to-make-it-big actors that meal is an important part of their day's food intake. Most of us don't depend upon our acting jobs to keep body and soul together.

When there are only a few extras, we get to eat with the "big kids". . . quite a treat.

Of all the production companies, John Hughes offers his troops the most generous meals. For example, when I was a hand double (someone whose hands are shown on screen in place of the hands of another actor) for "Curly Sue", dinnertime found us enjoying oysters (shucked by a Chef), fish, veal, and all the other trimmings and treats one would expect with such a meal.

The most original lunch I was served came with a surprising "side dish". As we extras were digging into our delicious Mexican meal (during the filming of "Red Heat". . . not a Hughes production), we heard the sounds of a mariachi band and, sure enough, in paraded the group dressed in their traditional garb. They serenaded us throughout the half-hour, and be assured that a happy group of extras went back to work on the mean streets of Chicago.

The only other meal experience that came close to this one was the time some crew members hired a sexy belly-dancer in honor of one of the guys whose birthday was that day. I've got to tell you that it wasn't the *lights* that melted the ice cream.

Much less often are extras allowed to share in the cornucopia of goodies spread out on the craft table. The craft table is *only for the cast and crew,* and woe be to those extras who take as much as a stick of gum from that bountiful groaning board. And bountiful it is. A typical craft table may contain several kinds of sandwich-makings, hot dogs, more kinds of candy, cakes and cookies than a diabetic should even *look* at, fruits and veggie trays . . . and the list goes on. These are just the between-the-meal snacks.

The most hurtful,, even insulting, occurrence happens when, between-meal snacks are offered to the cast and crew. Someone comes around with a tray of sandwiches, for example, and if an extra is standing between two crew members, crew member on the left of the extra will be offered the snack, crew member on the right will be served. What's the matter with this picture? The extra was passed by.

So we don't get a little sandwich; that's not polite, but what really bothers us is what happens during exterior shoots in winter and summer. Winter: Everyone is freezing. Here comes steaming hot coffee–but not for the extras. During summer shoots, substitute ice water–although water is passed to the extras if there's a chance that fainting from the heat might occur.

Oh yes, don't make the mistake I did the first time I was on an honest-to-goodness movie set. I thought that the honey wagon had something to do with meals. It doesn't–unless the food is *really* bad. So, although the makeup is kept in the makeup wagon, and the wardrobe is kept in the wardrobe wagon, honey isn't kept in the honey wagon. I'll let you, dear reader, find out what is.

After a few days of working on "Gladiator" (a boxing film), I would have liked to have said, "So long. See you around sometime." As it turned out, I stayed on until the last day . . . a bit over three weeks for the scenes I was in.

The location for the boxing scenes was an abandoned factory-type building in a seedy industrial section of Chicago. We were told that the place had been used to clean the motors of trucks, using some kind of strong chemicals. It was an old wreck of a filthy place, and many of us saw what we were sure was asbestos peeking out of holes around the structure. There also were flecks of "something or other" in the air and we were pretty sure it wasn't a gift from TinkerBell.

When we questioned the powers that be, we were told not to worry about anything because the place had been checked out by the appropriate City of Chicago authorities and seemed safe. So why were some of the crew wearing masks over their noses and mouths, eh? And strange, isn't it, that an inordinate number of extras became ill with respiratory problems? It cost an extra friend of mine a cool thousand bucks in doctors' fees and medications. Among all those extras, I was one of the fortunates who escaped whatever it was that felled so many. I guess we'll never know what secrets lurked within that dump because I was told that the day after the film was wrapped, the building was razed. It isn't called show *business* for nothing.

So why did I stick it out? I was selected to sit in one of the ringside seats, they liked my enthusiasm as I emoted for my favorite boxers. Since the leading man was named "Horn" in the film, that row was known as "The Horn Row". Later, when our row was needed, the call went out, "Will all the Horny people take their seats?" For the promise to show up everyday, all the extras in the front row were paid a bit more.

No way did I imagine that that job would stretch out so long. Things didn't start out as if the gods were looking kindly upon me. Coming home from the first day's shoot, at about ten at night, I was driving down one of Chicago's less desirable streets in a neighborhood decorated not with trees and bushes, but rather with winos and cement princesses.

Suddenly, it seemed as if the street had become even worse than usual. But it wasn't the street. I suspected a flat tire. Forget about stopping in *that* neighborhood to confirm my fear. Even though I knew it was unwise to drive on a flat tire, I just had to get to a restaurant area a few blocks away.

When I got there and finally took a gander at that tire, it looked as if it could have easily fit into the menu at the International House of Pancakes. What to do? Of course, I had to get help, but how could I summon the courage to walk into one of those eateries dressed up in

my weird outfit, topped off with a wild-looking wig, boxer fan get-up?.
There wasn't much of a choice, so in I went to that fine napery and
flowers on the table dining spot looking pretty much like one of the
winos in that neighborhood I had just left. After I explained my
predicament (and the fact that "I'm an actress and I was dressed like
this for a movie, etc". . .) the management allowed me to use the phone.
I called my road service, which responded quickly, but when one is sitting
in a nice restaurant looking like something that belonged in a dumpster,
the time went slowly indeed.

The following weeks on the movie, which starred Brian Dennehy
who most of us found to be a pain in the neck because he thought he
knew how to do everyone's job better than *they* did—including the
director and the fight choreographer—who's a recognized master, were
at once difficult and interesting.

I'm hard-pressed to determine which was worse on the "Gladiator" shoot—the toilet facilities or the food. Our toilets were portable
pottties, which were smelly, awful-looking and made us feel queasy. So
was the food. It was a draw.

The movie didn't get much play, but if you get a chance, rent a
copy of it; it's really pretty good. Try to find me in my different outfits
going goofy at ringside. I'm also in other parts of the film as a doctor,
but trying to find me would be like trying to pick out Waldo.

Little did I know when I was a student at Chicago's Navy Pier (the
Chicago branch of the University of Illinois before the U of I's Chicago
four year institution was built), that I'd be in a major motion picture at
the same place decades later. But that's the really exciting aspect about
life: it's the not knowing what's going to happen from one day to another. One *day* to another? How about one minute to another—or one
instant? And so it happened that one day I was booked to play some
scenes in "The Color of Money" at my alma mater, Navy Pier—which
by then was an abandoned hulk of a building which jutted out to Lake
Michigan.

For the film, it no longer was a leaking, run-down institution of
learning. It was a building at Atlantic City where a big billiards tournament was being held. Among the participants were Tom Cruise and (be

still in my heart) Paul Newman. Yes, Tom Cruise is adorable, but at *my* age Newman is, well, so smooth, so sexy, so . . . Paul Newman. It's not just those BLUE EYES. It's not just the fact that he makes all that food. It's not just his talent. It's that he's Paul Newman, who has been knocking me out since I was a kid of forty. And *I* was going to be on the same set with him. No matter that there were going to be hundreds of other extras there—so was I .

I arrived about a half an hour before my official call time. After parking my car, I checked in with the coordinator and made my way to the holding area—in this case a large bare room furnished with long, old wooden splinter-producing tables and folding chairs.

Sitting at one of the tables was a woman I judged to be about my age—or perhaps several years older. She looked pleasant and friendly, so I took a seat next to her, and we exchanged small talk . . . which included information about our adult children.

After giving her the names, ages, occupations and marital status of my daughters, I asked her to tell me about her offspring . . . two adult sons. "Do your children live here in Chicago?" "No, they live in California." "What do they do?" "Well, one of them is in the printing business, we're very proud of him." "And what does your other son do?" At that point she leaned over and whispered close to my ear, "If you promise not to tell anyone, I'll tell you: He's the director of this movie." That "second son" (not the printer) was Martin Scorsese—one of the masters of the business, who was directing Newman and Cruise in the film. Here was the mother of one of the acknowledged brilliant talents of our time: the director of "Raging Bull", "Mean Streets", "King of Comedy", etc., sitting in the common holding area with the rest of the extras.

Mrs. Scorsese explained in hushed tones that she'd like her identity kept under wraps because she didn't want to be inundated with glossys, resumes and scripts for her son (not the printer—the other one) to see.

Scorsese puts his mother and father in many of his films: In "Color" they were two of the high rollers.

For the days that we shot those scenes at Navy Pier, Mrs. Scorsese

was a joy to be with. She's a real down-to-earth lady. I kept my word. I
didn't say anything about Martin's Mom. Nevertheless, like a forest
fire in the middle of an especially dry California summer, whispers
spread about her. Even I got quizzed about what she was like, (could
she get some stuff to her son not the printer)?

As much as I enjoyed every day of my week on "Color", there was
one day in particular that tickled me pink—and made the other women
on the set green with envy. The scene: Paul Newman had just won the
first game of the tournament. As he was walking out of the auditorium
the crowd parted to let him pass. *I* was told by the a.d. to pat him
(Newman, not the a.d.) on the shoulder and mime, "*Great* game, Eddie!"
Of course, I was told just to *mime* the line. We all know why, don't we?
But who cared about money at a time like that? *I* was going to pat
Newman on the shoulder! I had to get it just right! I had to pat his
shoulder just as he was passing me, but make it look spontaneous. One
second I was to be applauding him, and the next second I had to pat
him on the shoulder and mime, "Nice . . . no *great* game, Eddie!"

My moment came. I did my thing as I was directed, although I
would have happily patted him somewhere else. That day I was the
Cinderella of the extras . The guys couldn't understand what all the fuss
was about. I've heard that even yet Paul Newman has not washed that
shoulder. I've also heard that Newman is planning to add marinated
platypus lips to his food line.

Among extras, if one of us gets a line—or even a special silent
bit—the rest of us rejoice for him or her. Most of us do. There are a
few extras who are as jealous as they come. But I think the green-eyed
monster is in residence in most businesses or professions. Isn't it?

There was one time, however, when even those "I shudda got
that" types were on the jealousy fence. They weren't sure if they wanted
the silent bit I got in "Vice Versa".

In the scene, Judge Rienhold is playing the drums in the instrument
department of a large store during the busy Christmas season. As shoppers
are running to see where the rock music is coming from, the camera
catches a woman of ample girth, with her backside facing the screen.
She's looking through a rack of shirts . . . and is really into the beat, as her

tush movements attest. Talk about having the guts to do a bit! I know, I know. Actors do all kinds of kinky things on the screen, and all I had to do was wiggle my clothed butt. However, when you're way over 21 and a cast and crew of more than a dozen people are staring at your backside, the moment can be less than glamorous. It wasn't glamorous, it was a bit embarrassing, it was also fun. I did it in only two takes—at the end of which I got a hand (not on my butt) from everyone on the set.

I also got some extra money for that silent bit. I've yet to figure out why extra money is paid for some silent bits (like the one above), but not for a silent bit like Cuban-nun-pushing-the-two-little-kids-in-a-wheel-chair-when-Ness-comes-up-and-talks-to-her. I think it has something to do with the fact that some production companies are so cheap that they'll get away with whatever they can. *They* know that we extras know that if we make a big deal out of not getting those few extra bucks we'll be seen as "trouble-makers"—and any extra who rocks the boat can be easily replaced. When it comes to extras, the lowest people on the movie-making totem pole they're the most dispensable of all the people. Picture a person with an industrial size cold; a box of tissues is at hand. He blows into a tissue, throws it away, and when he needs another one, there it is. Take one tissue—and another pops right up.

Why was *I* selected for that plum bit? I think that the director wanted someone who could fill up the screen. That didn't bother me; I was happy to have been selected for that funny bit of business. What *did* bother me was the fact that although only my back view was shown, all my friends recognized me!

This next experience, as of this moment, is the highlight of my years working in films as an extra and as a principal. One of the things that I find interesting about this particular experience is that it illustrates how a hunch, gut feeling, intuition, if you will, can make a big difference in your life. Sometimes you can plan what you're going to do and how you're going to do it for weeks. You put in a lot of effort and you get back zero. You just never know what's around the corner—and that's one of the things that makes life . . . life.

One summer day my friend Katalin and I went off in her car for a drive—the purpose of which was to pick up our airline tickets for a long weekend in New York City. The two-hour drive was worth it because we were getting some kind of half-price deal on those tickets. We picked the tickets up, and as we were driving back home, Katalin asked if I'd mind her stopping at a place a bit out of the way where they sold delicacies from her native Hungary. She's polite. I mean, it was *her* car, so you'd think that she could stop any darn place she wanted. What was I going to do, walk from the middle of nowhere back home? Of course I said, "Fine! You do your shopping and I'll wait in the car." After Katalin had been in the shop about ten minutes, something told me to take my new phone out of my purse and call home for messages on my answering machine.

There was a message from one of my agents. Upon calling him, I was asked if I'd be available for at least a week to work in a movie called "Dennis the Menace". I was selected as one of the gaggle ladies at the garden party. The problem: I'd have to report on the set during the week I was to have been in New York. The agent had to know no later than that day. What to do? Consider: It was a trip we had been planning for weeks. I had arranged the hotel accommodations. I was looking forward to the trip with Katalin—a woman I had come to know through our being extras in various movies. Those airline tickets were a great buy—and they weren't refundable. On the other hand, this was just extra work, and what the heck was a "*gaggle lady*"? Yet, through all of my "pro and coning" and my "back and forthing", a voice kept whispering, "Don't pass this up." Truth to tell, the voice wasn't whispering; it was shouting, "Hey, stupid, you can always take a trip to New York, but that five-day offer may not be offered again." I made up my mind.

I got out of the car, went into the shop and broke the news to Katalin as kindly as I could. While she was happy for me (although *she* didn't know what a gaggle lady was either), she was, understandably, disappointed about our trip. I offered to give her the fifty dollars it would cost to change the dates on both tickets. She graciously said she thought she could sell them to someone else. With her blessing, I called back the agency and said I'd accept the booking.

The first day on the set I learned that Walter Matthau and Joan Plowright, two of my favorite people in film, would be playing Mr. and

Mrs. Wilson. I also learned what a "gaggle lady" was in terms of the movie. I was to be one of several garden club members (gaggle) who arrive together at Mr. and Mrs. Wilson's home for the big garden party. Sounded like fun—but I had no idea how *much* fun. As it turned out, there were a few women too many who were sent by the agency as "gaggle ladies". Happily, I made the cut when director Nick Castle selected the few who he was going to use.

The scene started as the club members were arriving by car and foot. We "gaggles" were walking down the street arm-in-arm. In the next scene little Dennis, sees us, looks terror-stricken, and says "Cheek pinchers!". With that the "gaggle ladies"—and one "gaggle man"— descend upon the young lad messing his hair, pinching his cheeks and saying all manner of cutesy things to him. AND THAT'S WHERE THE REAL FUN BEGAN. THAT'S WHERE I KNEW I HAD MADE THE CORRECT CHOICE BETWEEN THE TRIP AND THE BOOKING.

The fact that I spoke in the scene, meant that I'd be paid a day player's rate, rather than the extra's rate I thought I'd be getting for the job. My "gaggle mates" and I were literally in the state of Illinois, but figuratively we were in the state of euphoria. Director Castle, and the director of photography both were pleased with our performances.

None of the "gaggle group" needed a car to get home at the end of that long, but happy day: we could have floated all the way. That was in August.

We weren't called back to continue the filming until October. Instead of an outdoor locale, the sets were constructed in a huge building in a northern Chicago suburb. Even that gorgeous backyard garden where so much of the action takes place in the movie was on the sound stage. I was placed on an aisle seat. We actors love to be placed on aisle seats; there's more chance of the camera seeing us—as it pans the audience. Since it took over a week to film that scene, the "gaggle group" became contract players which meant residuals *and* a SCREEN CREDIT. As we signed our contracts, our happiness knew no bounds.

The rest of my days working on the film were delightful, funny, insightful and, yes, ego-building to the max. When one is a contract player, one gets a trailer rather than a holding area. My trailer (and we're not talking U-Haul)—which I was to share with a couple of the other "gaggle gals", had a sitting area, a kitchen/dining area, a bedroom and a bath. Between takes I liked to sit there and read, away from the hurley-burley. I've gotta tell you that even though I wasn't a star—I felt like one. Oh, yes, I also got to eat off the forbidden—to—the—extras craft cart, although I never did that in front of my extra friends. We always got to eat lunch or dinner first, rather than last, as extras always do.

Taking a break in my trailer between scenes
for "Dennis the Menace"

Our hair and makeup got done first too. When the time came for me to appear on the set, a p.a. would come to my trailer to get me. Heaven, especially after years of being an extra, whose big perk was a cup of coffee and a Dunkin' Donut—if we were lucky. No one kicked me out of *that* trailer.

All of the above was frosting on the cake, great frosting, but not as important as the cake itself—which was being part of that movie. Unlike some stars, of lesser talents than Matthau and Plowright, those two went out of their way to be friendly with everyone, EVEN THE (GASP!) EXTRAS! Matthau would tell us stories between takes, and Plowright, wife of the late Sir Lawrence Olivier, was always gracious.

Once a group of us women were in the bathroom and one of the extras was complaining about a disliked agent (nothing terrible—just some kind of minor gripe). Just as she uttered an expletive, who should come out of one of the stalls but Ms. Plowright. The extra froze. Ms. Plowright said nothing, but she gave her a little smile as if to say, "Your secret is safe with me." As if Ms. Plowright cared about some Chicago agent—or what some extra thought about aforementioned agent. I think that the extra was embarrassed having used that kind of language when Ms. Plowright could hear it. The English star just makes you want to mind your manners.

On my last day on the shoot, to my surprise, Ms. Plowright gave me a hug and a peck on the cheek. She's not only an excellent actress— she's an excellent human being.

As one would expect from a John Hughes production, the premier night of "Dennis the Menace" was super, complete with red carpet, lights, refreshments and a smashing party afterwards. Hughes took over an entire popular Chicago restaurant. The food was super and *all* the children in the movie–even though most of those children were extras and extras generally aren't included in the parties–had a ball playing games and wolfing down a variety of "kid foods". The adults had their own room with more sophisticated fare.

As of this writing, I've earned thousands of dollars from "Dennis", counting my initial pay plus residuals. When this business pays off—it *really* pays off. Gut feeling, intuitions, hunch: they can really pay off, too.

Whether I'm a principal or an extra, regardless of whether I'm placed in front of the camera, or so far away from it that I need a taxi to get back to the holding area, I do the best I can to get into the mood of the scene. I knock myself out to bring, and to keep, a high level of energy no matter how long the shoot takes. It's the right thing to do for several reasons:

I'm being *paid* to do the best job of which I'm capable.

By doing my best I have more fun—and the time goes more quickly. [Did you ever notice the different attitudes among the people who collect tolls?]

You never know who's watching. Every so often, some lines are added during a shoot—lines that aren't in the original script. Who do you think is going to be given that line—or even that one word that the director thinks is important—someone he notices is full of enthusiasm or someone who's goofing off?

The director was highly respected. She had the reputation of being a no-nonsense woman who would settle for nothing but the best from those under her command. Make no mistake, "command" is not too strong a word. On a movie set the director *is* the commander-in-chief, whose lieutenants, no matter how proficient in their individual areas of expertise, must follow decisions of the big kahana. So here we have a strong presence in an industry that isn't known for its plethora of female directors.

In setting the scene the a.d. placed about six of us facing the camera. Surrounding me were attractive thirty-ish upscale types. I, too, was dressed in what's known as upscale casual, but the similarity stopped there. Age-wise anyone of them could have been my daughter. Weight-wise any two of those women probably consume fewer calories in a 48 hour period than I do in half that time. Hair-wise, they would have felt a home at an Junior League meeting. They were attractively coiffed—and as I recall most were blonde. My hair is short and silver. You can see that I wasn't a threat to any of these cutie pies.

My instructions from the a.d. .."Lee, walk straight toward the camera. As you get very close to the camera, veer to your left." Any extra would *love* that direction for the obvious reason that it would be considered excellent on-camera time. Unless the *direction* is to look into the lens of the camera (for a point-of-view shot, as I did in "Dennis the Menace") actors are *not* to look into the lens. What I had to do was walk toward the camera without looking into the lens. In order to do this I had to focus on a place either above the camera or on either side of the camera, but make it look as if I were looking straight ahead. This is called "cheating". Honest.

When the background cue was given I did what I was told until "cut" was called. Then I walked back to my first position and stood there waiting for the next background call. Suddenly, the director shouted, "You. The lady with the big glasses! Come here!" As I was walking toward The Voice, this quote rang in my head "Ask not for whom the bell tolls . . ."

Had I had a line I would have thought that she wanted to talk to me about a different way of delivering it. But all I did was *walk* as I was directed. Could it be that my eyes inadvertently glanced at the lens?

As soon as I reached her she said, in a brusque, but not unkind voice, "You're adorable." Nonplused I stammered, "I like you, too!" Talk about your clever retorts. She just wanted to tell me that I was adorable. I'm adorable? When my husband says I'm adorable, he says that because he sees my inner beauty. Actually his eyesight isn't what it used to be. When my daughters say I'm adorable, it's because they know that a will *can* be revised. When a *stranger* says I'm adorable, I'm at a loss to explain it.

As I write this the film has not yet been released. One never knows what will be edited out of the final cut. But, heck, what do I care? *I'm adorable*!

CHAPTER V

Short Takes on Big Stars

I've worked with so many stars over the years that I'd be hard-put to remember all of them. I wish that I had thought about keeping a journal when I first started working in films. Every now and then another memory pops into my mind—one that I had forgotten.

Here are experiences I remember involving people you have heard of. Some of these stars may be nicer than the experience I had with them led me to believe. Some of them may not be as nice as I thought. But, as the man said, "I call 'em like I see 'em".

TOM SELLECK The scene was a local airport for the film "Folks". Because the airport was across from a large subdivision, female fans were running like mad to see Selleck, and get his autograph, which the star declined to do. He did agree to have his picture taken with whomever wished.

I was standing on the sidelines watching the women as they had snapshots taken with the handsome hunk, and then saw them reluctantly leave weak-kneed and starry-eyed. Had the location not been in such a wide open space—practically impossible to "lock-up" (movie talk for securing a thoroughfare or any given area from auto or foot traffic while a scene is being shot), the "fan crowd" would have been cut down considerably.

After the photo fun had died down and only a lingering fan and I were standing near the star, Selleck turned to me and asked, "Don't you want to take a picture?" It wasn't said in a pompous manner, but rather in a way that showed concern for a lone woman who was holding back after dozens of other women had surrounded him. Leona:

"I'm one of the extras on this film. I'm not supposed to take my picture with you." Selleck: "Oh, come on. Go get your camera!" Leona: "I'm not supposed to bring a camera to the set." Selleck: "I'll bet this nice lady will take a picture of us with *her* camera. Won't you?" The woman, whom I'd never seen in my life, nodded her head in agreement. The picture was taken and, to this day, I find it difficult to convince anyone that *Tom Selleck* had to talk *me* into having my picture taken with him.

Can you believe that Tom Selleck insisted that I have
my picture taken with him? On location for "Folks"

DON AMECHE was a disappointment. I had been anxious to get to the set so that I could see him work. My "movie-fan impression" of him was as a kind and avuncular gentleman. In real life he made the Grinch look like Father Christmas. Indigestion? Or perhaps he was miffed because he hadn't made a cent out of his inventing the telephone.

DOLLY PARTON If Dolly Parton ever is the subject of a dirty "tell-all" article in one of those rags that passes as a newspaper, I'll be among the first to be up in arms. She of the big boobs and tiny waist is one of the few people in show business who truly is as pleasant on the set as she is when she's being interviewed on national television.

On the set of "Straight Talk", I was a resident of a seedy hotel, where Parton's character also lived. I was to pass behind her. As usually happens, the extras are placed in the scene and then the star is brought in. As Ms. Parton walked toward me to her mark she said, "Hi, darlin'. How 'ya doin'?" "I'm just fine," I replied. "How are you?" "I'm doin' just fine!", she said as she flashed a smile so broad, one would have thought she was running for political office. Since she spoke to me first, I felt that it wouldn't be inappropriate to say, "Ms. Parton. I've got to tell you that I've never worked on a film where the star was as well-liked by *everyone* as you are." "Well," she said enthusiastically, "aren't you nice to say that!" To which I replied, "You brought it on yourself. You've got only yourself to blame." She laughed. I laughed. And then the a.d. called "Action!"

I had no occasion to speak with her again, but watching her up-beat, friendly attitude with the cast, the crew, the extras and the fans who stood for hours across the street from our location confirmed my positive feelings about the lady with the Barbie Doll figure (except for Barbie's relatively flat chest) and a sunny personality that could make flowers bloom in the middle of the night.

ARNOLD SCHWARZENEGGER When Arnold Schwarzenegger was filming "Red Heat", he was a well-known film actor, but not nearly as well-known as he is today, so I wonder if he still is gracious when it comes to signing autographs as he was years ago.

TOM HANKS When Tom Hanks won an Oscar for his stunning performance in "Philadelphia" and another for his equally touching portrayal of the title character in "Forest Gump", I was happier than Madonna's bustier. Every once-in-awhile, not often, but every once in awhile, a nice guy finishes first—and from what I observed he *is* a nice, low-key guy–who I'll bet will get at least an Oscar nomination for his role in "Cast Away". Having just seen it, I'd **cast** my vote for his taking **away** the golden hewed fellow.

During a lull in the day's shooting for "League of Their Own", we were standing outdoors when Hanks remarked to me, "Isn't this a *great* day for an exterior shoot?" "Mr. Hanks," I replied, "this is Chicago; every day is gorgeous." With mock disdain in his voice, he shot back, "Lady, I've worked in Chicago—and, lady, you're lying!"

GENE HACKMAN One of the most physically demanding films for us extras was "The Package" starring Gene Hackman. The most difficult day for me and dozens of my colleagues was that bone-chilling-wind-that-would-knock-you-down-ice-and-snow-all-over-the-ground-kind-of-day that defied all our efforts to dress warmly enough.

We were filming a riot scene across from the Chicago Hilton and Towers. Because some of the male extras got *too* much into their rambunctious characters, people got knocked down; two young men required stitches. I found myself on the ground twice, and were it not for the "hoisting efforts" of two muscular young hunks, I would have been stepped on by a horse ridden by a Chicago cop. I was happy that my rescuers didn't end up being hospitalized with hernias.

When Hackman came on to the location, he said to a group of us, "Let's take a dip in the Lake [Michigan, which was a couple of blocks away]." "Since you're the star," I said, "you should be the first one in." He laughed and made a few humorous remarks which gave us just that bit of "warmth" we needed to keep our spirits up.

He's a celebrity who isn't loath to give autographs. I understand why some stars don't. They don't want to be bothered, think autographs are silly, they're preoccupied thinking about their lines. What some stars don't realize is that to many people, that piece of paper with a simple signature is their connection, however flimsy, to a world they perceive as glamorous. Even many of us extras have been asked for our autographs by on-lookers: A little girl once told me that getting my autograph on her birthday made her day "perfect!" May she always find joy in such small pleasures.

ELI WALLACH Here's an actor who, as far as I'm concerned, never has worked as much as he should have. In addition to his considerable acting talent, I had occasion to see another facet of his personality.

It was one of those horrible winter evenings into which one wouldn't send that proverbial dog . . . but we were extras. About halfway into the night, as we were taking a break indoors, I was sipping a cup of hot cocoa, when Wallach's soft, kind voice inquired, "Are you warming up? Are you O.K.? It's very cold out there, isn't it? The cocoa warmed my body; Mr. Wallach's words warmed my spirit.

CHRISTOPHER LLOYD aka Switchblade Sam in the film "Dennis the Menace", is an actor who is much better looking than the roles his fans have seen him in. One day I had the pleasure of spending about 10 minutes talking with him over breakfast. Friendly, relaxed, with seemingly no "star ego", I got the impression that he's the kind of guy who'd stop to help a stranded motorist change a tire . . . even if that motorist were an extra.

BILL MURRAY The round trip between Woodstock, IL. and my brick ranch in Naperville, IL. is about 110 miles (not as the crow flies—as a car goes).

Woodstock, IL. was the location of the smash film "Groundhog Day", starring Bill Murray. I worked 24 days on that movie and found Murray to be a fellow who enjoyed talking to us about baseball (he's a great Cubs fan) and often made us laugh as we stood around between takes. The poor fellow certainly didn't enjoy the time one of the groundhogs nipped him.

Some time after the film was wrapped, those of us who had put in many long—days on "Groundhog" received an autographed picture of Bill & Phil (the groundhog). No big wow, but a thoughtful gesture nevertheless.

DANNY DE VITO didn't endear himself to the dozen or so actresses who had an 8:00 P.M. call for a "looksee" during the filming of "Hoffa". I got to the location a little before eight, was directed to a holding area, and there I, and the other hopefuls, sat for well over four hours until Director DeVito took time out to look at us. We had gathered for the purpose of his deciding which of us would get the non-speaking role of a waitress in a diner scene. One of the women got so tired of sitting around that she wanted to leave; I convinced her to stay.

Finally, after he had his dinner, he spent less than 10 minutes to make his selection. The gal who wanted to split got the part. When the film came out you could hardly see her. What really got us angry was the fact that DeVito looked at us via a small TV from a couple of blocks away, and never walked over to thank us for coming—as most directors do. [Note: Had I been selected for that bit, I wouldn't have been available to work on "Dennis the Menace".]

CUBA GOODING, Jr., one of the actors in "Gladiator", a boxing film, was a sweet-as-they-come young man who I predicted was going places in the movie business. Looks like I was right. During the filming we exchanged a few words (I from my ringside seat, he from the canvas of the boxing ring). It looks like his celebrity hasn't tainted what appeared to be a truly nice human being and that he'll remain "a man of honor.".

MAUREEN O'HARA was a favorite with both the young and the "more mature" members of the cast, crew and the extra contingent during the filming of "Only the Lonely". The young admired her for her graciousness toward everyone. The older members among us remembered her from our own youth—and found her to have lost none of her magnetism.

The stars of the "O'Hara Era" had a certain something that can't be bought or taught. Implants won't do it nor will liposuction. Ya either got it or ya don't. O'Hara's got it.

MADONNA Her style isn't my cup of tea, but on the set of "A League of Their Own" I observed a quiet, friendly woman who seemed to be well-liked by her co-workers. And who knew that *ROSIE O'DONNELL*—who also appeared in the movie would become a big-name talk show host before too long?

KATHLEEN TURNER, the personification of sunshine, burst on to the cocktail lounge set of the film "V. I. Warshawski" with a smile for everyone. Before long she went over to where a group of us extras were sitting waiting to be called to our marks. She sat talking with us for about fifteen minutes, about how she never was an extra (never wanted to be) but how she appreciated the work that extras do. Extras don't often hear *that* coming from a star . . . especially from one who means it.

SANDRA BULLOCK Although she obviously takes the execution

of her craft seriously, this adorable star of "Speed", "While You Were Sleeping" and "Miss Congeniality" seemed more like an unspoiled, carefree college kid when I saw her on the set of "Sleeping". Some movie mavens predict that she's going to take the place of Julia Roberts in the popularity polls. I've got the feeling that Bullock would happily settle for peaceful co-existence.

RICHARD GERE Having worked in Gere's film, "Primal Fear", I'm delighted to report that the consensus among the female and male extras was, "He's even more handsome in person than he is on the screen!" He has the kind of "Paul Newman" good-looks that reflect intelligence as well as physical attributes. So stunningly handsome is he that the director had to remind us women that in the scene we were supposed to act as if we hated his character. That, my friends, was *acting!*

A couple of other "hunks" whose reputations among us extras is ☆ ☆ ☆ ☆ are Mel Gibson and John Travolta.

GIBSON loves to play good-natured pranks. He's also been known to sit and, not only talk to extras, but play a board game or two with them. Some of my friends have had lunch with him on location for "What Women Want" and were impressed with his down-to-earth personality.

TRAVOLTA is a sensitive, considerate man who sees to it that extras get the same food as everyone else and he too, isn't above exchanging a few pleasantries with them.

SUSAN SULLIVAN What a difference there is between Dharma's haughty mother-in-law, played by Susan Sullivan on TV's "Dharma and Greg" and the real-life Sullivan. She was a dear during the filming of "My Best Friends' Wedding", pleasant to everyone as far as I could observe. At one point she turned to me and said, "Sometimes I forget to stand nice and straight. If you notice my posture beginning to slump, give me a signal". And that's what I did. From time to time she'd look over to me and I'd either give her an O.K. index finger-to-thumb-sign or, on just a few occasions, throw my shoulders back. She'd flash me a smile and form a silent "thank you"

ERIQ LASALLE As he walked on to the outdoor set for an "E R" scene in Chicago's Loop, squeals of joy were forthcoming from both the young and the more mature fans who had gathered to watch the filming. He is, indeed, a handsome gentleman who, unlike many male stars, looks bigger in real life than he does on screen and he's better looking too, in my view.

I was sitting at the edge of the set waiting to be called for the next scene as LaSalle walked toward me. When I smiled he asked me if I liked being an extra. I replied that I love doing background work, and that I've been doing it for a long time. "That's the important thing–to love what you do", he enthused. Oh, how I wish I had had the nerve to have added . . ."and another important thing is to make many thousands of dollars *while* you're doing what you love"

JULIA ROBERTS Working in the film "My Best Friends' Wedding" for 20 days could have been a blast. As it turned out, it was a bust.

It was hot most of the time, the mosquitoes were having a catered affair with us extras as their entrée. Our meals were fair on the good days–fowl on the other days.

The changing area was dirty and contained only two chairs for dozens of us women. Putting on panty hose while standing on one leg may be easy for a flamingo, but not for a female extra.

When we had to move from one building to the next we had to side-step mud and the ruts in the road. All in all it wasn't one of my pleasant adventures in movieland.

Roberts has a radiant smile. Too bad she chose not to share a bit of that toothy grin with us extras. It would have been a gracious gesture during those tedious weeks. She wasn't mean, but she sure didn't go out of her way to give us a morale boost.

More often than not we extras exchange amusing or sweet little stories about how one star or another acknowledged us with a "Hi! How are you doing?", "Like your scarf", "Nice Day!", "You guys sure are working hard!" None of that with Roberts, as far as any of us heard.

Seems to me if one is a big star in the Hollywood firmament, it wouldn't be a sacrifice to share just a bit of that glow with us mere mortals below.

WES BENTLEY During the filming of a funeral scene in "Soul Survivors" a pleasant young man asked me if I'd like to take his seat until shooting started.. I answered, "No, thank you, I'm fine standing". He insisted that I rest, if only for a few minutes. Because he was such a gentleman, I finally took him up on his offer.

At lunch later that day I mentioned what a pleasant fellow he was. "Don't you know who that is?" asked an extra. "Who?" "Did you see 'American Beauty'?" "Just last night," I replied. "Remember the next door neighbor?" "Of course. He was a cute kid." "Well, that 'cute kid' is Wes Bentley—the same 'cute kid' who offered you his seat this morning."

GEORGE CLOONEY Sure he's handsome as they come. But is he a good guy? He sure is. Point in fact: During an "E R" shoot in Chicago's Loop two of the extras told me they were going to ask Clooney if he'd pose with them for a picture.

I told the college kids that they'd get into trouble because, as they knew 1) Extras were not to approach the principals, 2) Cameras weren't allowed on set, 3) If they did the first two, they were sure to get, 4) FIRED. They assured me that they didn't care if they got fired–*after* they got their picture with Clooney.

The next thing I knew Clooney was inviting them into his mobile home where he posed with them and exchanged a few pleasantries. Late into the evening the young men still couldn't get over their good fortune.

KATHY BATES Years ago when I worked on the film "Prelude to a Kiss", in which Kathy Bates was one of the principals, I got the impression that she was a shy, quiet woman.

Years later when I worked in the film "Unconditional Love", I saw a self-assured, friendly actress. It's remarkable how stardom can raise one's confidence quotient. After a long scene, she walked along with several of us extras and told us what a good job we did and how much she appreciated our efforts in the film.

It was the first time a star walked me to my holding area. O.K., so we just happened to be going the same way, but for a while she really seemed like one of us.

BURT REYNOLDS and Sylvester Stallone When the movie "Driven" was being shot at the Chicago Motor Raceway in Cicero, IL, both Burt Reynolds and Sly Stallone starred.

Look at the two hunks I "adopted" while on
location for the autoracing film "Driven"

The consensus among the extras was that Reynolds would be stand-offish and that Stallone would be the good-old-boy of the duo. We were wrong, as we learned from people who saw what happened. Reynolds was congenial–even posed for pictures. Stallone was unfriendly–even a bit hostile when a fan approached him with a "Hi, Sly!". So, kiddies, today's lesson is: Not *all* stars twinkle.

ANTHONY EDWARDS "E R" star Anthony Edwards was direct-ing. Before the next scene, he instructed, "Leona, I want you to start your cross-over when I give you a little poke". [Sometimes extras start their movements with other than the background call: a pat on the shoulder, a visual signal or a silent count are all used]. "Fine", I re-plied. Wanting to be positive that I understood, he added "Maybe I'll give you two pokes, O.K.?" "You can give me *three* pokes and I won't tell "The National Inquirer", I joked. With that, he smiled and said, "Then what good is it?"

WALTER MATTHAU When I learned that I'd be acting in a scene with Walter Matthau in the film "Dennis the Menace" I was *pleased* because I had admired his talent over the years. I was a bit *nervous* because Mr. M. played a curmudgeon so convincing I wondered how close that persona was to the real-life Matthau. I wondered, too, if like some stars, he was so full of himself that he'd be a royal pain. As it turned out, he was an absolute joy, a Teddy bear, a funny, friendly gentleman whose face was a delightful kaleidoscope of expressions.

Between takes he told us amusing Hollywood tales which our small gathering listened to as intently as a group of kids during story hour. When I mentioned that I had seen "The Sunshine Boys" some six times, he said that the George Burns' role was to have been played by Jack Benny. Benny died, Burns stepped in to take his place.

Matthau then took a gold money clip from his pocket–a gift from Benny. It was engraved with that "39-year-old" violin virtuoso's profile.

Walter Matthau passed away in July 2000. I like to think that Walter and Jack are starring together, at last.

CHAPTER VI

You Meet Some of the Nicest People– and Some Others Who Are– Don't Ask–I'll Tell You

A movie set often is like a small town—with its myriad of different people from all walks of life and various personality makeups. Some of those people I'd love to have as neighbors—some of them I'd love to have on another planet.

The person who has impressed me the most is my friend Katalin. Her life would make a fascinating movie—more exciting than most of the films we have been in as extras. Katalin came from a well-to-do family in Budapest, Hungary. She lost all but a few relatives during the Holocaust. The man to whom she has been married for over fifty two years, is the same young U.S. Army corporal who helped liberate her. Knowing Katalin has given me the opportunity to learn history from someone who survived one of the world's most horrific outrages.

Sam's a retired surgeon, in his 80s. His sons have a fit every time he works as an extra. We were doing an exterior shoot on a lovely spring afternoon on Michigan Avenue—just a group of shoppers and business people—part of a scene for one movie or another. I was paired with Sam and as we walked along he whispered, "I sure hope one of my sons doesn't catch me doing this." How do you like that! A man in his 80s worried that his adult children will catch him playing with the other kids! I guess what goes around really *does* come around.

There's a couple, whose names I'll not reveal, who are examples of every extra's worst nightmare: They are basically good people, but, whenever they can get away with it, they hog the camera. If the a.d. puts them in a spot that they deem too far from the camera, inch by inch they creep to a more visible venue, even if it means getting in the way of another extra. Sometimes the rest of us make book on how far they'll get before their transgressions are discovered by an assistant director.

To those who think extras knock themselves out for the money, I'll tell you about a couple who live on Lake Shore Drive—also known as the Gold Coast of Chicago. . They were offered something in the area of a thousand dollars a day by a film company for the use of their high-rise apartment as a set for a movie. They turned down the opportunity because they didn't need the money and they didn't want to take the chance of their floors being marred by all the equipment that's used during a filming.

Of course, if any damage occured, the production company would have made any repairs necessary. Whenever a production company rents a house, apartment or place of business, the fee paid is generous and the cast and crew respect the property. If any alterations have to be made (different wallpaper, paint, carpeting), the owners, at the end of the shoot, have the option of leaving the place as it is or having it put back to its original state. Even though the Gold Coast couple declined that bit of walking around money, the last time I asked, they weren't on food stamps.

Big Bob, not to be confused with Bob the Trouble-maker, is a retired sales rep who stands head and shoulders, literally, above any crowd. Good-natured, Bob always is fun to sit with in the holding area because I love to hear about all the trips he and his wife take. I know a *lot* of world travelers, but I know of none who have set foot upon more foreign soil than B.B. and B.B.W. (Big Bob's Wife)—who, by the way, was thrown off the set of "The Untouchables" when an a.d. thought she was looking into the camera. She wasn't looking into the camera (a major no-no), but once an a.d. decides an extra has broken one of the rules, there's no arguing the matter.

I guess no matter where one works, there's at least one person who can't get along with the rest of the group. Among us Chicago extras, there's a woman who seems to get her life's blood by being as unpleasant as possible. She feeds on arguments with the same zest as a junk-yard dog feeds on a hefty slab of meat. And, like a mean-spirited dog, she snaps at every little thing . . . real or imagined.

During the filming of the TV series "The Untouchables" I was standing with other extras in a line waiting to get my hair done for that period piece. Most of us were schmoozing while waiting our turn with the hairdresser. Out of the blue, "Miss Congeniality" walks up, gets in front of my face and declares, "I'M BEFORE YOU!" "How do you figure that?" "Because I was here a little while ago—so don't try to get ahead of me!" Who could argue with *that* reasoning?

It's better, with this piece of work, to let her have her way—especially over such a petty thing. I will say this for the witch: she's an equal opportunity cantankerous character. I've seen her vent her spleen time and again with no regard to age, race or country of origin.

The only time I can recall her speaking in an upbeat mood was when she was relating the tale of how a director she met in Italy promised to make her a star: "He said I have great cheek-bones". I'm not saying that the director *didn't* say that he liked her bones, cheek or any other part of her skeleton. What I am saying is that she can't expect people to give a hoot about any of her victories real or imagined when she's just as likely to tell you to go to hell a few moments later because she thinks you said or did something she considers an outrage.

I know of at least two agents who no longer will book her; she's not worth the hassle. There simply isn't time on a busy set for trouble-makers. Cooperation is key.

An extra friend I get a kick out of is Reba, the widow of a long-ago well-known Chicago radio personality. In her 70s, she's the epitome of the society matron whose bearing and dress make her right at home in any scene that reeks of elegance. But "snooty" hardly describes Reba. In the middle of any given conversation, she can come up with a naughty bit that one wouldn't dream could be uttered by this silver-haired, bejeweled stately woman.

Are extras dumb for working so hard for so little money? I introduce you to Betty, a member of Mensa and a woman who came in second on "Jeopardy". Betty speaks several languages and knows a little about almost everything. She's also smart enough to know that there are some things money can't buy.

Kind, gentle Sey, a retired insurance rep, is more ready to listen than to speak. If there's anyone who doesn't like him, he or she is keeping it quiet. Sey, and a myriad of others, make holding areas considerably more user friendly.

Adding to the friendliness of holding areas is the fact that most extras are more than happy to share tips for getting acting jobs. Thanks to just such generosity, I got a line on working as a mock patient at the University of Illinois medical school in Chicago.

Networking resulted in my signing with an organization that provides actors for mock trials at one of the Midwest's most respected law schools.

My murder mystery jobs also came about through the grapevine. Acting jobs are hard to come by; there are so may more actors than there are gigs. This is what makes the sharing that much more meaningful and kind.

We were sitting in the shade of a building in Chicago's Loop between scenes. The young woman and I had struck up a pleasant, if innocuous, conversation. She ws unaffected and soft-spoken as we waited in our outdoor holding area. After a while, she said, "I just have to tell someone: My daughter is up for a part that's very important. We'll know soon if she got it." Nancy Chlumsky soon found out that her daughter, Anna, did indeed, get that part—opposite Macaulay Culkin in "My Girl". You just never know who you're going to meet on a shoot.

During a commercial filming at Wrigley Field, Dennis Franz was featured. At that time he was one of the stars in the TV hit series "Hill Street Blues". The world had not yet had the thrill of seeing his behind sans underwear.

During a break I was chatting with two sisters who, like me, had been working as extras. During the course of our conversation they asked my name. "Toppel?", said one of the women, "Are you any relation to a Marilyn Toppel from Maywood?" "She's my sister-in-law," I replied. "We went to school with Marilyn! We *wondered* what happened to her!" With that, she called over her brother and said, "Dennis, this is Leona Toppel. She's married to Marilyn Toppel's brother! Mr. Franz exchanged a few pleasantries with me and then it was time to get back to work.

That encounter brought together high school friends—and—as a matter of fact my sister-in-law, who is married and had been living in Los Angeles for many years, had dinner with the sisters and Dennis Franz when the women visited their brother in California.

What I got a kick out of was the story that was revealed later in the day about Franz: It seems that when little Dennis was only three he was to have spent the night at my in-laws', but he cried so much for his mommy that he had to be taken home. So much for that tough detective of "NYPD Blue".

Not to be overlooked is the fact that among the doctors, the lawyers, the CPA's, the singers, the fire fighters, the students, the homemakers, the sales reps, the truck drivers, the artists, the writers, the photographers, the wealthy, the poor who may be found in a movie holding area, there's no generation gap. Young and old work together, eat together, talk together with, generally, good humor and mutual respect. Because I'm usually the senior member of the extras assembled, many of the young adults ask my advice about various aspects of their lives. One young, sweet actress asked, "Leona, how can I get equality with men?" To which I answered, "Why would you want to lower our standards?" On another occasion a first-time extra asked me if I thought that she'd get a line during the day's shoot. "Sure you will," I replied. "When dinner time comes there'll be a *big* line. Get into it. Yes—you can find even a philosopher among us.

Variety? You'll find it in the extra's holding area. So the next time you go to the movies be aware that that drunk you see in bar scene may be a minister in real life. That bank robber may really be a police officer. The young woman playing a hooker, may be a preschool teacher . . . or a hooker.

Dennis Franz during a break on location at Chicago's Wrigley
Field Before his buns made their glorious debut on "NYPD
Blue". With extras Vera and Leona.

CHAPTER VII

Did I Get It or Did She Get It?

Some people say the odds are one in fifteen. The optimistics say the odds are one in ten. Whether an actor wins one in fifteen auditions or one in ten auditions he or she goes after, if an actor wants work as a principal—or even as a supporting player, he or she must audition. After all, if Meryl Streep auditions for parts, who are the rest of us to turn up our noses at the process?

Those numbers of one in fifteen and one in ten don't mean that, after going to fifteen or ten auditions you'll win one. Would that it were so. The other side of the coin is a bit brighter. Every now and then an actor will go to several auditions in one week—and win them! My "personal best" was three for three in one week. The next time that happens, I'll be looking skyward–to see all the flying pigs.

Generally speaking, I enjoy going to auditions. I find them challenging, I like seeing some of my competition, and best of all, I like getting the booking—as do all of us who try out. That's why I laugh inwardly when I hear Actress A wishing Actress B, "Good Luck!", as Actress B leaves the waiting area to go into the room where the auditions are taking place.

Perhaps I'm not the most talented actress at a given audition, but regardless of how I speak the lines, I don't speak out of both sides of my mouth in the waiting room.

In a nutshell, here's what happen when you get called for an audition: You're told the character you'll be portraying, the date, time, place of the audition, the shooting date and sometimes the fee. Most of the actors I know don't ask what the fee will be; we trust our agents to make the best deal for us.

Never, ever, ever give an agent—or anyone else—one red cent to get you a job. No honest agent will ask you to pay him or her anything until you get paid. Should an agent ask for a "pre-job" fee or a fee for having your pictures taken and printed, fly like a UFO from that agent's presence. Go to an independent source to have pictures taken.

Now that we've got that out of the way, let's continue with the audition adventure. You'll arrive *on time* or five or ten minutes early to "get yourself together"; it's not wise to rush in out of breath and a nervous wreck from fighting traffic or looking for a parking space.

After you sign in, you'll get a chance to look over the copy and the story board. When your turn comes, you'll be called into the room in which the director, and sometimes the clients, are seated. More often, someone from the casting company will run the audition. You'll be asked to "slate yourself" (say your name and the name of your agency).

After you're finished performing your audition lines before a video camera, the individual behind the camera will say, "That was *very* good. Thank You!" or just "Thank You", or "That was *perfect*!". Don't, for your own sake, read anything into the "That was *very* good" or the "Thank You!" or especially "That was perfect!". Many times I've heard a "That was perfect" that was so enthusiastic visions of residual checks floated before my eyes. On many of those occasions, I didn't get the job. At other times, a simple "Thank You" resulted in, you guessed it, my getting the booking. You'll get a call after the audition *only* if the job is yours: It's a "Don't call us, we'll call you" situation. And they *mean* it. By the way, unless instructed differently, dress upscale casual (no jeans).

Getting back to those who run the audition: Some of them could not be friendlier, trying to put you, the actor, at ease during the audition. Others make those faces on Mt. Rushmore look like regular "softies". But don't mistake anyone's facial expressions as a barometer of your success–or failure–at the audition.

I had an audition with a director who fell into the latter group. It's easier said than done, but try not to let the crabby ones out there get to you, because there are a lot more of those pleasant types around to make up for the meanies.

Some of my favorite directors, David, Mel, Russ, Neil, Kevin are the kinds of directors who make you feel that, in spite of the fact that you're an actor, you *can* have something worthwhile to contribute to your performance. I love to have the opportunity to improvise a bit and most directors will allow it, if the information isn't lost and the time restraints are respected.

When you go to an audition, put your best foot forward and should that foot just happen to get caught in your mouth, know that it's not the end of the world. There will be other auditions—and the first time *you're* the one chosen you'll know that all of the previous "didn't get it" disappointments were worth that victorious "I got it!"

One of the most often heard phrases in the business is "Don't take it personally". Difficult as it is to swallow, someone else just may get the role that you want not because that actor is more talented than you, but because he or she (1) *looks more* like "the type" that the client or director envisions than you do, (2) *looks less* like someone that the client or director *doesn't like*: e.g.—a teacher or not-so-loved relative, (3) just happens to "click" with the director or client personality-wise. Since these are factors over which you have no control—there's no point worrying about them. So again—if you win the audition, re-joice; if you don't get the booking, don't take it personally.

Typically, actors like to take jobs that will allow them to be absent for a couple of hours so that they can go to auditions. Popular "I'm-doing-this-until-I-become-a-star" jobs include working in the food service industry, clerking and "temping". I demonstrated products in stores, and it was this employment that opened another door for me. As in any job you never know when or where an opportunity will come along, so give your best to whatever job you're doing, because you just don't know who's watching. More about this later.

CHAPTER VIII

Safety First! You've Got to Watch Out for *Lots* of Things in This Business

You've probably heard a performer being wished that he "break a leg". Break a leg? Why in the world would anyone wish such bodily harm upon another person? In point of fact, the "break a leg" wish started during Shakespearean times. When taking their bows, stage performers would bend at the knee or "break a leg". While "breaking a leg" on stage is good, breaking a leg literally is bad—so is spraining an ankle—or getting hurt in any other way–whether on a movie set or going to and from the location.

The first time you're on a set, you'll notice how much equipment is all over the place—and with the equipment comes all manner of electrical cords which cover the floor like a pit full of snakes. Catch your heel on one of those cords and there's the potential for a big time accident. So, as the farmer said in the cow pasture, "Watch where you step". Although every effort is made for safety on a set, accidents do happen—usually out of carelessness.

On the set of "The Color of Money", about 500 of us extras were returning to our assigned seats after our lunch break. Most extras are gregarious—and I'm part of that not so silent majority. I was preoccupied talking with a friend as we mounted the steps to our bleacher perches where we were playing spectators at the big Billiards Championship games. A misstep caused me to fall. Falling in front of a couple of people is embarrassing enough but taking a flop before 500 people—most of whom

I didn't know—was humiliating. The only positive aspect about the entire episode was that so many people showed concern—which also proved to be a problem. Several people were "helping" by pulling on my legs, several other "helpers" were pulling on my arms. "Where's the paramedic?!", asked others. "I don't need a paramedic," I said—trying to take some measure of control—which wasn't easy when with each passing second I felt more and more like a beached whale. The paramedic *did*, indeed, check me out: I was suffering from a serious case of injured pride. On every large production set there's a paramedic, but even on small productions, there's someone in charge of the first aid kit. Here's hoping you never need even so much as a Bandaid.

Danger can come from the most unexpected places. While working on a music video I was playing a secretary. Just a few moments after I left my desk, a huge piece of equipment crashed where I had been sitting. My agent for that job happened to be present, and seeing my near disaster, she broke into tears. Who says agents don't have lotsa heart?

Your safety is *paramount* (not to be confused with Universal, 20th Century Fox or Warner Bros). Don't let the stress of what goes on during a filming get to you. You can be sitting in the holding area for *hours* from your call time—and then, like a bolt of lightening, the call rings out, "We need background NOW!" Sometimes, with that urgent request, comes the order to change into different wardrobe. So off everyone rushes to put on other clothes, while trying to get to the set in under a nano second.

At that point, no one gives a hoot if guys and gals are changing next to each other. Most of the time, rest assured, changing rooms aren't unisex. Because everyone is so occupied with throwing together what they're going to wear, peeking isn't a priority.

Don't rush so much that, if you're on the way to an outdoor location, you dash across the street without paying attention to what might be coming at you. Carelessness could make you the star of a call to 911. Look out BELOW, AROUND and UP if you want to leave at the end of the day on your own.

The worst accident I've had, so far, happened. not on the set, but on the way to an audition. It started out great: I found a parking spot only three blocks from the casting office . . . .a stroke of luck on Chicago's busy streets.

Walking to of my appointment, I was crossing the railroad tracks and suddenly found myself sliding across the blacktop on my face. The force was so hard that the lenses of my glasses had traces of tar etched into them. During my life I've experienced pain of that magnitude only four other times: one was when I tore the cartilage in my knee, and the other three times resulted in the birth of three human beings.

Two men, passing in their car, saw me, ran over, helped me up and asked if they could take me to the nearest emergency room. Although I was bleeding from my face, knees, and the palms of my hands, I refused, explaining that I had to go to an audition. They drove me the remaining two and a half blocks; I could have sworn I had slid at least that far.

I arrived at the audition on time—looking as if I had gone a couple of rounds with a food processor-and the food processor had won. It so happened that I was auditioning for the part of a tough old gal. I guess my banged up face impressed them because I got the part. What we actors do for our craft!

When you're down and out it's
good to have influential boyfriends.

As an extra you'll travel all hours of the day and night, so it's important that your car is in tip-top condition: tires, oil, transmission fluid, brakes, battery, full tank of gas. If you can swing it, have a phone in the car and know which emergency numbers to call. There are few things worse than having your car break down on the way home from a shoot—unless it's having your car break down on the way *to* a shoot. There's only one acceptable reason for your not getting to the location on time: a death in the family . . . *you*.

It was a winter night, during a snowstorm, way past midnight. Sitting in my car I felt as if I were inside one of those large glass globes—the kind that you shake to see the pretend snow flakes swirl all over the little snowman. All this would have been beautiful—if I hadn't been alone—and lost. In the winter an early morning call takes me out in the dark and brings me home in the dark. It's at times like that that I feel like a Welch miner. I stayed calm and finally found my way to a familiar street. The next day I bought my first cellular phone. But no matter what, it's best not to panic.

Don't bring more money than you absolutely need for phone calls, transportation and a charge card, all of which you'll keep with you on the set, but *do* bring some cash

For a cheapo Korean production, we were told we had to buy our own lunch because unlike the USA, Korean actors buy their own meals. Our agency rep talked them into springing for lunch—which they finally did from McDonald's, which we ate on the curb . . . during a misty, gray half-hour break. The fact that we were dressed in those ridiculous hospital nightgowns, didn't raise our spirits.

If our agency rep hadn't been able to talk the big spenders into popping for one small hamburger each plus one can of soda, I would have needed a couple of bucks to buy some nourishment.

All the dangers in this business don't lurk on the set or going to and fro: People sometimes can be more dangerous than piles of cable, cords and heavy equipment. I can tell you, from experiences, that being hurt by unethical people can leave more "bruises" than bumping into a tripod or falling down a few stairs.

Remember that time when I got three jobs in one week? Two of them were from being sent out by the same agent. I completed both projects, received compliments from the directors and the clients on both films, I waited for my agent to send, first the check for the job I finished at the end of February, and then for the job I worked in April.

Because it usually takes several weeks for the client to pay the agent—and then for the agency to take its commission and send the remainder of the fee on to the talent, I wasn't concerned when a month passed and no check was forthcoming.

About halfway into the second month, I called my agent to inquire about payment for the first job; I was told that the client hadn't paid them. I called an excess of a dozen times, and got the same story, which actually turned out to be a fairy tale.

Winter turned to spring. Same story. As spring was going into summer, everything was turning green—but *I* wasn't getting any of that green with the presidents' pictures on them. Finally, I did something I hadn't done during all the years I had been in the business: I called the clients and found out that each of the two had, indeed, sent the checks for my services months before.

The agent had been using my money and telling me that she hadn't been paid. It took well over a year—and out of almost $1,300 I recovered 23 cents on the dollar. Why only 23 cents on the dollar? Because dozens of other actors had been stiffed too when the agency closed its doors. There's just so much to go around from the bond money that the state requires agencies to put up.

Although most agents with whom I'm associated are hard-working, honest people, there are a few out there who cheat actors out of the monies due them either by using the fees for their own expenses or claiming that the client has cheated *them*.

It's lousy when unethical agents cheat *anyone* out of monies due them, but it really angers me when they pull those stunts on young, struggling actors who need the cash to keep body and soul together. The landlord isn't about to wait months for the rent.

So watch where you step, watch where you drive. and watch your back.

[Note] Even though I lost a lot of money on those two jobs, something good came out of one of them: I was the principal in a video made for Lutheran General Hospital in Park Ridge, Illinois. Titled, "Mrs. Dorothy Peterson: A Case Study, Health Care in Crisis", it was produced as an in-house tool for discussion among the staff. It ended up as a finalist in the International Health and Medical Film Festival, and is currently being marketed to other hospitals. I got a mention in a widely read movie industry magazine—a boost for any actor!

As you have noticed, watching your step in this business refers to various areas. You can trip over cords and cables . . . and your own words. I've done it.

Unlike some people who get into trouble when they're in a foul mood, I get into a jam, once-in-awhile, when I'm feeling "up". It seems that the happier I am the more talkative I become, the bolder I become.

On location for "Losing Isaiah", we extras and some crew members were packed into what had to be the world's slowest elevator as we were returning from our dinner break.

As sometimes happens, we background people didn't know who the director was, so I asked the pleasant looking young man in the jeans and the bright yellow tee-shirt, "Do you know who's directing this thing?" At that, all the crew members let out a howl. Smiling, the fellow replied, "I am".

Ye gads, why did I refer to the movie being shot as "this thing"? No one let me forget my goof for the remainder of that long night of shooting. Some wise-guy even shouted, "'This Thing', starring Jessica Lange, coming soon to a theater near you!"

Another of my "accidents" took place, not with a crowd surrounding me, but rather between me and just one other person. When actors meet on location there's happiness in the air, regardless of where that location happens to be, because they're working. That was the atmosphere when I arrived to do an industrial film.

A couple dozen people were standing around swapping the latest show business gossip. Some true, some worthy of "The Best of the

Liars Club ". Among the group was a fellow who was joining in with his share of laughs and stories.

Later, when he was standing alone, I approached him and said, "You look familiar; I think we've worked together. How have you been?" "I'm fine", he replied, "and we *did* sort of work together. You auditioned for me last week. I'm the director". CALL 911! SOMEONE IS DYING OF EMBARRASSMENT!

As I later recalled,:the day of that audition was a couple of weeks after my eye operation and I didn't have my corrected lenses. Add to that the fact that the director was sitting off in a dimly lighted area of the room—plus the fact that his mood on the day of the audition was different than it was on the day of the shoot. The man had gone from a bear to a lamb. To his credit—and my relief—he was a good sport. He even gave me a line during that day's filming.

CHAPTER IX

Sparky and Friends

"He could get work, when there was a call for tall men, as an extra, but he hated the thought. Extras weren't actors, they weren't even human, they were movable props. Actors and actresses were protected from the rigors of film-making; extras were dispensable. If they passed out from the heat of the high, hissing arc lights, or went half-blind from the lower Kleigs, or threw up from the nauseating green glow of the Cooper-Hewitts used for full illumination—oops, replacement, please, and roll 'em. Extras never got near the director, only one of his assistants. They didn't talk to the principals. They weren't addressed as people; 'atmosphere' or 'background', the a.d. would call when he wanted his extras' attention. Extras stood around all day, many a tedious day, waiting for some kind of action. Actors lounged in canvas chairs, at a discreet distance from the peasants, made jokes, talked dirty, had a drink brought on a tray, got a neck rub, called everyone endearing names. An actor was what Clark [Gable] wanted to be, not a prop." (From "Long Live the King" by Lyn Tornabene)

Two extras, Shirley Kelly and Roseann Krevitt, came up with an idea to bring Chicago extras the recognition they deserve. Kelly and Krevitt gave birth to an award they named Sparky. The "gold" statue, about as tall as an Oscar, is mounted upon a dark wood base and has a modern feel to it. A hole in its tummy enables one to peek through at the "background".

Since it wasn't possible to award the Sparky based upon the same categories as the Oscar, it was decided that any extra who so desired could write about his or her funniest, most frightening, happiest, etc.

experience while working in a movie. Each submission was assigned a number in place of a name in the interest of fair judging. The most interesting or/and amusing tales won Sparkys at a "black tie optional" cocktail party. The presenters weren't Hollywood luminaries, but rather Chicago radio and television personalities who participated in the festivities with enthusiasm.

It was quite the affair, always held at a top-notch Loop hotel, and one that many of us looked forward to eagerly each year. Alas, rising prices brought to an end the Sparky fun and games. I won a Sparky which, for the past few years, has been standing on my desk waiting for an Oscar to join it. Fat chance.

Even though the Sparky competition is no longer part of the extras' social scene, I've asked some of my friends to pretend that they're vying for one of the little guys. There follow some first person, true adventures of background artists, some of whom are waiting for that big break, all of whom are "star-quality" people.

MORRIE ABRAMSON: I was working in the TV series "Crime Stories". It was a hot summer day and between takes I was sitting on a step of this old tenement where the show was being shot. An a.d. came by and said, "Please move; you're in everybody's way". After she said that, but before I had a chance to move, she kept looking at me and then she spoke into her walkie-talkie, "I think I found a corpse". Apparently, I was it. "Let's go upstairs so the director can take a look at you", she said. I'm 79 now, and I was no kid then, so I said, "If I have to walk way up there I *will* be a corpse".

Well, I was O.K.'d for the corpse and I was made-up on the sidewalk with everyone looking on. Pretty soon the call came, "Ready for the corpse!" So up I walked into the tenement and up those stairs. I made it! I was put into one of the apartments and the door was closed upon my reclining form.

The next thing I knew two "detectives" burst into the room and discovered the "corpse". At that same moment a big flock of pigeons was released and flew over me. I knew I couldn't move, but I sure felt like it! Lucky for me, the pigeons didn't leave anything on "the corpse"— and I earned a hundred dollars for laying down on the job.

A really nice thing happened when I was working on "The Color of Money". In the scene I was to follow Tom Cruise into a pool hall. Unlike the "Crime Stories" shoot, this one took place on an ice cold day. It really surprised me when Tom Cruise asked if he could get me a coat. I said, "No thanks", but then seeming to be concerned about me, he asked again. Again I said, "No thanks".

It's nice to know that someone you admire as a talented actor is also a thoughtful person in real life.

KATALIN ZAMIAR: I was looking forward to the day's shoot for "Richie Rich". I love to get dressed up—*and* I love my prize whippets. This shoot was going to be a combination of both:

I was told to dress very upscale and to bring one of my dogs for a scene which was going to take place on Chicago's Gold Coast . . . very ritzy! I'd be walking along all dressed up with my dear pet at the end of her upscale leash.

As I was waiting in the holding area, in an exclusive private school, one of the school's officials told me I couldn't bring a dog into the building. Well, I sure wasn't going to wait out in the cold with her, so I quietly sat with the wardrobe people in their room, which was fine with them because they were dog-lovers and welcomed giving shelter to me and my dog Onyx.

As sometimes happens, a scene is changed at the last minute, and that time *I* was the one they didn't need.

So instead of walking along the Gold Coast with Onyx I was assigned to put on a *very downscale* sweater over my *upscale* outfit, get into my rusted 1986 Taurus, put Onyx out of sight in the back and follow a pizza delivery truck in which the film's star Macaulay Culkin was riding.

During one of the backups, the truck struck my car and did six hundred dollars worth of damage—which the production company said they'd pay. What an end to a day that started out so happy! But, hey, I'm an extra, I'm tough, I can take anything.

JOHN NICOSIA: When I got my first commercial I had *one line*: "Little lady wanta buy a car?". I was so nervous I could not remember that line. It came out, "Wanta buy a car?", "Little lady want a car?",

"Little lady buy a new car?", "Little lady how about a car?" After about six or eight times the director changed the line to "Hey, little lady want to buy a car?" I was so screwed up I said, "Come on little lady; I got a car for you". They kept that one. In almost 12 takes I *never once* had said the line correctly. The other actors asked me why I kept changing the line. I fibbed, "The director wanted to see what line he liked the best".

PEGGY WOOD In May 2000 I was working on the Mel Gibson movie "What Women Want". We broke for lunch and walked from the set to our holding area, which was a vacant restaurant [generally the holding area doubles as the dining room].

I was sitting at a table eating with some other extras when I noticed that Mel Gibson and his family were seated at the table behind me. Our backs were nearly touching. Oh, joy!

After awhile I heard a sound. A disgusting sound. The loud disgusting sound of a bodily function. The kind of bodily function sound favored by adolescent males. At first I thought that Mel might be having a digestive problem . . . even though the meal was quite good. As the noise continued to anger me, I turned to give Mr. Mel Gibson–big star, God's gift to women–a dirty look. When I turned, what did I see? I saw a sweet doting father holding his baby while making "raspberry sounds" against the infant's bare tummy. While I felt guilty for my assumption, I *did* learn something: Believe what you see with your own eyes, not what you hear . . . especially in the movie business.

DARBY ISAACS: I was working in "Straight Talk" with Dolly Parton doing a party scene. We extras were directed to look like we were having one heck of a good time . . . to really laugh it up. Well, I love to laugh even when I'm *not* before a camera, so when I heard "Background action!" I laughed like I never laughed before. Of course, in the making of a movie you keep doing the same thing time and time again, so I had to keep laughing like mad during all the takes.

At the end of the scene, Ms. Parton came over to me and said, "Darby, you're so much fun I'd like to have you come to one of *my* parties!"

I'd love to say that that was exactly what happened: the party was great and *I* was the most popular guest there. That's what I'd *like* to say . . . except that I never have been invited to her home. But I like her anyway; she's a sweet, kind woman who was admired by everyone working on the film.

HARVE KOLZOW: How can one express an "outstanding experience" in the entertainment business when you're involved in working with the likes of the Queen of Movies, Maureen O'Hara and the late John Candy in "Only the Lonely", the talented Joe Pesci in "With Honors" and Macaulay Culkin in "Home Alone", the brilliant directing of Andrew Davis in "The Fugitive" and Ron Howard in "Backdraft" and watching the expertise of the stuntmen in the boxing scenes in "Gladiator?". Each and every opportunity I have been fortunate to be a part of is an "outstanding experience" in its own way.

However, the most unique experience would have to be working ringside as the timekeeper for endless hours on a hard wood bench in "Gladiator". I was too engrossed and too macho to think of comfort and thus am permanently tattooed with black and blue symbols of dedication on my rear end as a souvenir. There will always be anticipation for future "outstanding experiences" as long as I'm able to continue being a part of this fascinating business.

GEORGE BECKER: I have two experiences which stand out in my mind as a movie extra. On "Next of Kin" with Patrick Swayze, I was one of a group of 30 extras working on a el train scene on the near north side of Chicago.

We broke for lunch at a small church near the elevated train station. We were told to assemble after lunch at the Armitage el station for further instructions by the coordinator. We were all standing around the coordinator listening to instructions, when someone yelled "Lookout below!". All of us were startled and did not know what to do. For some reason which, I will never know, I took one step forward as a 50 lb. electric drill came crashing down from the station platform above to the ground in the *exact spot* where I was standing. Had I not taken this one step forward, I would not be here. I thank my lucky stars every day.

Another memorable experience was when I worked on "Mo Money" with Damon Wayans at Water Tower Place. I was assigned to be a bookstore manager, so I thought wearing a fake mustache would make me look more academic and dignified. When Damon came into the bookstore, he walked over to the window display. I was told to walk over to Damon, and ask him if I could help him. During our exchange Damon said, "Your mustache is coming loose; you better glue it back down". Fortunately it did not fall off, and nobody else mentioned it to me.

JIM SBARBORO: I was working in the movie "The Package" with Gene Hackman. The scene I was in was the Governor's Luncheon at the Hilton Hotel in the Loop. I was playing one of the governors and had all my crew with me, plus my "wife". There were about 50 tables each seating 10 people as well as a long straight speakers table on a raised platform.

As we were standing in line to be seated, I saw two cameras on a platform opposite the speakers' table. When our group got up to the assistant director, he pointed to a table for my group to be seated. As we were walking towards the table, I kept my eye on the cameras and as I got to the table, I picked the seat facing one of the cameras. As the rest of the group sat down, I noticed that none of them thought about the position of the camera. It was in back of them. I thought to myself: "They must be new at this, or they just don't care" [about being seen on camera].

After everyone was seated, I felt great that I was in camera range and at last I might be able to be seen in this movie—for a change. My "wife" remarked: "Don't they look real?". "What looks real?", I asked. She pointed to the cameras. "They are real", I said. She persisted: "I know they are real *cameras*, but they are going to be used as TV cameras and *extras* are going to *pretend* that they are taking picture with them". "Where is the real camera?", I asked with a sick feeling. "In back of you", she replied.

FRAN WASCHBUSCH: I always wanted to play a nun in a movie or on television. During a segment of "The Untouchables" I got my chance. I was sent to wardrobe where I was fitted for my habit. Well, I wasn't exactly "fitted"... it was more like "ill-fitted". I'm only five feet tall, but the only nun's outfits they had were for taller—much taller—women.

Wardrobe did the best they could. They pulled, they tucked, they pinned. When they got done, much of the costume was bunched around my waist. I thought I looked a bit like a pregnant penguin, but no one else seemed to notice. What *was* noticed was the length of the sleeves. If I kept my arms criss-crossed and tucked them into the sleeves, they didn't look *too* bad, but whenever I put my arms to my side I looked like one of the Seven Dwarfs.

All through the shoot, whenever I was needed on the set, the call went out, "Get the Dopey nun!"

WILLIAM GOLDBERG: In the movie "Straight Talk", I was given what most extras would give their eye teeth for: A line! All I had to say was "Goodbye, Dr. Shirley! I love you!" Dolly Parton was Dr. Shirley— and *I* was shaking with fear. I just couldn't get it out. My wife, bless her, was working in the scene and she was trying to help me get over my fright. Can you imagine a man's wife trying to *get* him to say "I love you!" to Dolly Parton?

I decided after that embarrassment I never wanted to work on another movie; I was afraid that I'd *get* another line!

PEGGY DAVIS: Because I live in the city I don't have a car, which means that I generally can accept movie jobs that are accessible only by taxi or by public transportation. So when my agent called and said that there was an extra job for me about 10 minutes from my apartment, I was happy to take the assignment.

Loaded down with my wardrobe I took the elevator down to the lobby to get a cab. The weather was horrendous: pelting rain, and wind blowing like something out of an old South Seas film. As I looked out, I saw a woman being blown down. The doorman tried his best to keep me from going out, but I was determined to get to the shoot.

I finally got a cab and arrived at the location, an office building. I was soaked to the skin from the short time I was outside getting the taxi and then, to add to my discomfort, I was selected as one of the workers who would be standing on the escalator *all day*. The problem was that I *hate* riding on escalators. I never step foot on escalators. I'd rather walk to the top of the Sears Tower than to take an escalator. But that was my assignment . . . so I rode on the darn escalator *all day*

That awful shoot had its "ups and downs" in more ways than one . . . and even the "ups" were downers.

REBECCA HOGAN: I got into the movie business after I retired from the hotel industry. Being an extra isn't always easy. One time, in order to get to a shoot I had to get up at three in the morning to catch a 4:30 A.M. bus.

Another time, three of us couples had to run down a Loop street . . . through an open fire hydrant! And how could I forget the firemen who trained their hoses on us!

Then there was the time four of us were trying to get to a location via a "no-man's land" empty lot. We were climbing over all kinds of junk—including barbed wire. In the process, I cut my leg, and when I got to the location someone stopped the bleeding with hair spray!

Life without being an extra must be dull.

JACK BREWER: Although I have worked for years as a singer and stage magician, my first experience as an *extra* was at eight years old; I played a little boy in a movie entitled "The Golden Glove Story". I was paid candy and other goodies for my work. At that time candy seemed like enough.

Throughout the years I have been in over 50 television shows and movies: I was in the big parade scene in "Ferris Bueller's Day Off". In "Mo Money" I played a drunk (I rehearsed by staggering around the house). In "Flatliners" I had to bump into Kevin Bacon on the elevated train

After those silent experiences, I *finally* had my big chance to actually *speak*: I was directed to "shsh!" Maureen O'Hara, one of my favorite actresses. I thought, "Maybe, just maybe I was going to get my 'BIG BREAK'".

Director Chris Columbus told me to "shsh!" her and then she would turn around and tell me off. That was really an awesome experience for me because I grew up enjoying her movies. The scene was cut.

I told the director that I didn't feel bad about being put on the cutting room floor with the likes of Roddy McDowell—who was also in the same cut scene as me. Mr. Columbus said, "Yes, Jack, but he made a hell of a lot more money than you did".

I *did* have a speaking part on a TV series as Mr. Roebuck. I was a drunk Santa in "Miracle on 34th Street" and a wacky scientist in "Richie Rich".

Maybe some day I'll get my "BIG BREAK". If not, I know I had a "BIG PART" in the movies, because you can't make a movie without extras . . . and have it look real.

ELISABETH NORTH: Some of the wardrobe personnel, especially the ones brought in from out of town, have very "creative ideas". Since we live in Chicago, we know what is normal and practical to wear in our town, but it does not always please the crew chief.

One particularly memorable lady, Leslie, came along with a production company from Toronto. Most of the made-for-TV movie had been shot in Canada, but since the story was set in Chicago, they needed some exterior shots for local color: elevated tracks, Wrigley Field, views of the Hancock Center.

I was told to bring the following wardrobe for the day:

1) Blue-collar scrubwoman, taking the el to work.
2) Casual attire to wear to a Cubs game.
3) "Nice" dress, not too dressy, to wear to dinner.

We were all warned that Leslie wanted what I call P.T.C. (Pack the Closet), *lots* of choices. My instructions were to show up at the Wrigley Field el stop as a scrubwoman. Leslie didn't think my shapeless brown-flowered dress, run-down shoes and hair in a bandanna looked authentic. But I lucked out: They came through looking for someone my height to stand in for—of all people—Robert Young, and I was out of there.

The afternoon was not so lucky. None of my T-shirts, shirts and sweaters pleased Leslie, who wanted to see what else was in my garment bag. She selected a pink pastel dress as appropriate to wear to a baseball game! Whatever they do in Toronto, a dress was not my idea of what Cub fans wear, and I felt awkward surrounded by sweatshirts, T-shirts and tank tops heading for the park. Since she had selected the best dress I had with me for casual use, I worried about what she would want for dinner wear.

Lucked out again: Since they thought they had used me enough that day, I got sent home early. What a shame I didn't get to see more of Leslie! I'm sure she would have wanted me to wear my brown-flowered "Cleaning Lady" sack as a dinner dress!

JOHN L. BELLAZZA: For the film, "Running Scared", with Billy Crystal and Gregory Hines, I not only was an extra, I also was the "funeral director". I didn't *play* a funeral director, but I *did* provide the mourners and the altar boys for the cemetery scene. Because the scene was an Italian funeral (which, by the way, was filmed at a Jewish cemetery) and because I'm of Italian extraction, my agent asked me if I could round up a group of suitable mourners and altar boys for the occasion. I did that by calling my relatives, who were pleased to appear in a major motion picture.

As a result, everyone in the scene, with the exception of Hines, Crystal and the priest, were related to me. I've got to tell you that Hines and Crystal treated my entire family as if they were *their* family; they were great to them. Unfortunately, my family and I had a lot of practice going to funerals over the previous six years when we had several deaths among us.

I also helped the director teach the actor/priest how to properly cross himself and how to handle the religious objects. We did the scene in only one day—rather than the two days the director thought it would take, so he was one happy man. My family and I were happy too, because *this* time we were getting *paid* to mourn!

EMMA CARLINO: My lifetime dream to be in a movie—or even just on a set was to become a reality: I was going to be an extra in a movie called "Date Night"!

I planned my wardrobe carefully; I was to be a spectator at a hockey game. I brought everything out of the closet and carefully tried each one on, hoping to capture just the right look. I could hardly sleep, and when I dozed, I dreamed of being discovered

I woke up very early and prepared for the momentous occasion. All shiny and excited, I set off for a northern suburb to a hockey rink.

We were all checked in, our wardrobe approved, given our vouchers and told to guard them with our lives. They would be turned in at the "wrap" and we could be paid only when we gave them in after a full day of work.

The lighting—cameras and sound man—and all the crew, it was so enthralling, for a while. After six hours of sitting in various places on a backless bench, in a freezing hockey rink, as the cold seeped into my very bones, it was a delight to break for lunch.

Eleven hours and I *still* wasn't discovered. Freezing, back aching, wondering where was all the glamour, I finally was part of a group called upon to make a "cross" (to walk into and out of the scene) in which the two main characters were fighting with each other. We weren't to notice and just act as if we were on the way to the ladies room. We were lined up along the wall and the assistant director started giving directions on where everyone should go. Unfortunately, I was in the far corner amidst a sea of smoke, under hot lights where I could barely hear and could not see at all. I presumed as we came closer to the "cross" I would be instructed to go left or right. As my turn came, and I could see the area to be crossed for the first time, I was nudged at the shoulder with no further instruction.

I stepped out and prayed I would go the right way. Just as I crossed in front of the actors, the booming voice of the director shouted "CUT! SHE WENT THE WRONG WAY!" His sentence reverberated around the cavernous hockey rink. Everything stopped dead. All eyes were riveted upon me, the sinner. My heart stopped; I thought for a moment I might expire on the spot.

We were told to go back to "one". Go back to our beginning spot. I did so amid the "tsk's" of my fellow background artists to await my judgment. I was sure I was going to be told to leave and never return to a movie set for as long as I lived.

The a.d. came rushing over to ask who was the culprit who went the wrong way. I was almost in tears. I said "I'm so *very very* sorry". I tried to explain and I apologized profusely, showing him my real anguish. Seeing my earnest and genuine sorrow at "messing up" he took my hand in his and said, "It's all right. That's why we have rehearsals. Just don't do it again". I thanked the Lord for another chance.

After twelve and a half hours we turned in our vouchers and went home. Although I hadn't been *discovered*, I still felt the call of the movies and knew I'd do it again and again.

CECILIA SCHWER Like so may extras who have had the pleasure to have worked with Mel Gibson, I, too think that he's one really nice down-to-earth guy.

He was sitting with a group of us at the Chicago Athletic Club during a lunch break. The movie was "Payback", and we were delighted that he wanted to spend part of his "off time" with us. The conversation was lively. When I asked him if he had ever been an extra, he answered with his usual frankness, "Thank God, No!

DONNA HOLMES I *love* the challenge of being in the movie business. It's never the same, you just never know that's going to happen next–like *this* adventure.

About a hundred of us extras were dressed in formal attire for the party boat scene in "Unconditional Love". Our dinner break took place at a building under Michigan Ave. in Chicago (you never know *where* you'll be having dinner). We were ushered into the place via a service door and into a freight elevator (who says making movies isn't glamorous!) So 30 of us were standing there–the "beautiful people", women in jewels and lovely gowns; the men in black tie. And surrounding us were mops, brooms, dirt and darkness.

Then the elevator got stuck between floors! All dressed up and no place to go. Being "brave little extras" we hardly panicked at all. After awhile the elevator moved, the door opened and we were free at last, although we felt a tad less glamorous.

So far the highlight of my movie career took place when I was asked to be a stand-in for Kathy Bates in the film "Unconditional Love". Being there every day, getting to know that Kathy Bates, who besides being an outstanding actress, is also a gracious, kind woman. One of the great things about being a stand-in is that you're right there, close up and personal. Being the stand-in for someone like Kathy Bates was a thrill. I'll never forget it.

DOT BROWN While having the good fortune of working in a high budget movie I met many very dedicated people, among them the person responsible for the wardrobe. This man had the most remarkable memory of anyone I had ever met. He could remember every article of clothing and jewelry on each of several hundred people. I learned just how good his memory was first hand. I was dressed for a formal scene—gorgeous gown and jewelry. We did several rehearsals and then we were given a 20 minute break.

After the break I took my place on the set, when all of a sudden, out of the blue, the wardrobe man rushed toward me with a horrible look on his face while screaming, "What's that ugly black thing on your arm?! You were right in front of the camera with that ugly black thing on your arm!"

He scared me to death. I looked at my arm expecting to see some disgusting crawly bug. What I saw was my watch—with a black band—that I had slipped on during the break so that I could keep track of the time and forgot to remove it.

But he noticed . . . and I was chewed out for forgetting one of the commandments of movie-making: Thou shalt always pay attention to continuity.

Sometimes extras learn the hard way.

JUDY CARMEN I admit it: I love being in the spotlight, but in this business with all the competition, it's not easy to get a job. We've all had our disappointments. That's why I was so thrilled when I auditioned for a commercial and got the booking. For weeks I carefully planned what I was going to wear, how I'd fix my hair, my nails and makeup for the big day. I studied my lines. I was one happy actress . . . until the night before my big day . . . when I fell. I was rushed to the hospital with a broken ankle. I'm not sure which pain was worse: my broken ankle or my broken heart. There was no way I could do that commercial. Goodness knows I tried to have them schedule it for another day. It wasn't feasible—and they never called me for anything again.

Things were looking up when I read in the newspaper that "Charlie's Angels" was having a nation-wide audition. When they came to Chicago I went to the cattlecall and the casting agent didn't even give me a chance to show him what I could do, but later that week a friend in New York City told me that they were coming there and that I should try again. When I arrived at the call there were thousands of potential angels all over the place. When it was my turn to meet with the five judges they asked me what I enjoy doing and what I'd do if I got the role. That night the call came from their casting agent giving me the news that I had been selected as one of the ten finalists! After the call back I and four other women remained in the running. What excitement . . . for awhile. By the end of the week they called and said that the entire project had been canceled. Another disappointment! But I still love acting because there are many more exciting happy moments then disappointing ones–like

· When I was a scrub nurse in the film "Soul Survivors"
· When I worked on "What Women Want" for four days and stood just two feet from Mel Gibson
· When I auditioned for the part of a nun in "Dragonfly" and I *didn't* break my ankle the night before, it *wasn't* canceled and I got to work next to *Kevin Costner*. Life in the movies can be reely great!

SALLY LOEB "Home Alone" was my claim to fame! I played a passenger in a scene that took place in a mockup airplane cabin. The camera started out on me, went over my head and stopped on Catherine O'Hara. It's then that she realized her son had been left "home alone".

During the year the movie came out–and after annual re-realeases–total strangers would ask me if I was the woman in that scene. I felt like a true STAR! People even requested my autograph.

This is just one of the experiences that make being a movie extra worthwhile. Here's another one:

Kevin Costner, star of "Dragonfly", was filming in a Chicago residential area. I saw him walk over to a group of about 25 neighborhood people, who had come to get a glimpse of him on the set. He came up to the group, introduced himself, and said, "I would be happy to sign autographs but in doing so all you'll see is the top of my head bending down, so let's talk first." Wow, was I impressed! He told us what "Dragonfly" was about and asked if anybody had a question for him. After questions were answered and autographs were signed, he said–"Who wants to have your picture taken with me?"

Never before have I seen or heard of any actor taking the time and trouble to be so accommodating and thoughtful towards extras and others looking at the movie making. Costner did this 3 or 4 times during the 12 hours of filming that day. All I can say is "Hats off to Kevin Costner."

CHUCK GRENIER: During the filming of "Stir of Echoes", starring Kevin Bacon, another extra and I were cast as security guards. We were to pass metal detectors over Kevin Bacon and two of the actresses as they entered a football stadium. What a great bit! I held them by the shoulders as I passed the metal detector over them. Then an a.d. told me not to touch the actors—at which time Kevin Bacon said, "It's O.K. if you put your hand on my shoulder". This was the first time a big name actor spoke to me; it made me feel great.

"Which one of you has the line?", the director asked the other security guard and me. Neither of us knew anything about a line. There was *one* but only *one* line in that scene. Since only one of us could deliver it, the director said that whoever won the paper, scissors, rock game would be given the line. With that, he held up his fingers in a scissors motion. Unfortunately, I had never heard of that game (obviously a defect in my childhood education) so I figured that the best thing I could do would be to mimic the director. I held my fingers like he had—and so did the other extra . . . three times in a row. Finally, the director said one of us would have to change or we'd be there all night. We both knew he wasn't kidding. Reluctantly, I did the scissors motion again, and the other extra switched to the rock gesture which made him the winner (because, as I found out later, rock breaks scissors). If only I had known how to play that darn game!

As I looked down at the crowd of extras in that scene, many of whom I knew, I could see the disappointment for me on their faces. Later they came up to me to say how sorry they were that I didn't get that line. Only another extra could "feel my pain". Ironically, the winner was a newcomer to the movie business and didn't have a clue as to the importance of getting that one line until we told him about the initial pay raise, the screen credit and the residuals.

Several years later, extras still come up to me and ask, "Hey, Chuck, have you learned to play paper, scissors and rock yet?" Sometimes they just hold up their fingers in the scissors motion. I just wave at them and laugh–because in this industry, disappointment is the price of doing business–whether you're an extra or a star.

Although I've had my share of good silent bit parts, I used to think that that security guard line was a once in a lifetime chance that would never happen again. But, you never know. There's always a next time. When you're an extra "hope" is always part of your personal script.

SEYMOUR R. PLOTKIN: Since March 1986 I've been in a number of feature films, made-for-TV movies, stand-in jobs, etc. One of my most memorable events occurred during the making of "Opportunity Knocks" in 1989.

The scene was a bar mitzvah celebration which was being shot outdoors at a posh estate. The director, Donald Petrie, selected me and another male extra to do a bit as guests who nearly come to blows in a furious argument. Petrie liked our work and at the end of the day he had us signing contracts, we were told that residuals were in our future. I was elated. This feeling stayed with me until I saw "Opportunity Knocks" at a sneak preview:

Lo and behold. I caught only a *glimpse* of myself at the lawn party. The rest of the scene landed on the cutting room floor. There went my hopes of being a "movie star". But even though there were no residuals or my name in the movie credits, I *did* receive a nice check from Hollywood.

I also loved working in "The Package" as a Russian diplomat, as a truck driver in "Hoffa" (where it was a thrill being directed by Danny DeVito—and meeting Jack Nicholson) and as a cardiologist in "The Fugitive" (even though we didn't wrap until four in the morning).

Like anything else in life, being a movie extra has its highs and lows. But when you become part of the film-making process, it has a way of getting into your blood. Oh, there are many tedious hours of just sitting and waiting, and there are countless rehearsals and retakes, but I wouldn't trade the feeling for anything else. I'm only sorry I didn't start in the business in my younger years.

CHAPTER X

Show Biz Kidz

Is the movie/TV business child friendly? That depends upon three major factors: the child, the child's parents and the child's agent.

Child: There are many cute children on this planet (and for all we know, on other planets). There are many cute *and* smart children on this planet. But when we are looking for cute, smart and willing-to-follow-direction children the field is narrowed.

Know, before we go further, that "cute" doesn't always mean a curly-headed, dimpled darling. "Cute" comes in all shapes, sizes and colors. "Cute" includes personality and pizzazz. "Smart" doesn't mean Einstein in a mini-body. What's desired is a sharp, "catch on quickly" type who, and this is essential, is not only bright enough to catch on, but has enough self-confidence to take direction without hanging on to mom's or dad's leg or curling up on the parent's lap like a prize Siamese pussy cat. Before you offer your offspring to the film gods, ask yourself if your pride and joy goes ballistic if he doesn't get his way, if he stiffens up like a frozen carp when a stranger talks to him, and if told to come here and then sit there will stay there . . . or run around like one possessed.

There are few businesses in which time and money are more important than in the movie/TV industry. Consider: In the making of a movie or television film, dozens of people are involved besides the director, the talent and the camera operator (never confuse the camera operator with the director of photography). There are grips, gaffers, make-up and wardrobe people, teamsters, usually some extras, caterers. Even on low budget non-union projects we're talking about at least four or five people behind the camera.

You can understand the frustration on a set when a unmanageable child is holding up the proceedings. Remember Anthony? When infants are involved, twins are generally employed because little ones may be on the set for only a short time and because if one child is acting up, the replacement can be brought in.

Every time a child will not cooperate, the action must stop, but the clock keeps ticking. The director, cast and crew are patient to the nth degree, but there *are* limits.

Parent: As the parents of your potential star, you'd do well to ask yourselves why you want your child to get into the business. Is your motivation to have your child do what you wish you could have done when you were a youngster? Have you heard stories about how much money can be made? Has your child been begging you to be one of those kids who sell soda pop or cereal? Can you manage to take your child to last minute calls for auditions while still caring for your other children? Can you afford the pictures, the clothes and other related expenses?

Can you, yes, *you*–not the child–take the rejection? 'Cause no matter how cute and talented your darling is, there will be times when the booking won't go to your team.

Do you have reliable transportation needed to get you and your child to out-of-the-way venues? There are a lot of locations not accessible via public transportation.

These are just some of the concerns you'll have to face–concerns both husband and wife must agree upon–if you value the most important concern of all: Are you willing to put your family's well-being at jeopardy for the chance, and I repeat–the *chance*, that one member of your group will find fame and fortune?

Macaulay Culkin was the star of the blockbuster "Home Alone". The adorable blond-haired youngster was the talk of the movie world. What insiders knew was that Mac's dad was a controlling, drunk, abusive brute. Lucky for Mac that by law 90% of his income was placed in a guarded account until he turned eighteen. Culkin revealed that as a child he never had a vacation, never had a full year of school (although tutors are on locations where there are children involved).

According to Culkin, his father's abuse got so excessive that he called the police. Culkin's mother hasn't been with his father for a long time, the senior Culkin has disappeared–and the son has no desire to see him. Mac said that his dad was interested in him only when he was making money.

For a study in contrasts, consider Mason Gamble, whom I had the pleasure of working with in "Dennis the Menace". In the role of the title character, Mason was just a regular kid when the cameras stopped rolling.

Several years later I met him again on the set of "E R". That particular shooting day was Mason's birthday. There was a large cake, balloons, we all sang "Happy Birhday" and Mason and I, in commemoration of the cheek-pinching scene in "Dennis . . ." pinched each other's cheeks while a picture was taken. He seemed like a sweet, happy kid.

Mason Gamble and I doing the pinching bit during his
birthday celebration In the holding area while waiting to go
back to our work on "E R". [Note] This was the coldest day of
the year so I layered, layered, layered.

Certainly, a major factor for his mental health has to be his healthy family life. When I worked on "Dennis . . ." I spoke on several occasions with Mason's father. During our conversations it was obvious that the Gamble household was a far cry from the Culkin disaster.

So while there are examples of children and show business successes (include Shirley Temple Black in the positive column) there are, I'd venture, many more instances of unfortunate endings. Sit in the waiting room of any place where auditions are taking place and several children are trying out for the same part and you'll get quite an education. Some parents act as if the child who did less than a star-quality audition (or at the last moment decided he or she didn't want to "shine") had committed a heinous crime. Lucky for most children, the parent's attitude is "I'm sure you did your very best, honey. Now let's go have lunch!"

Agents Almost every agency has a department that deals with casting children. Some agencies deal *only* with casting youngsters. But whichever agency you decide to work with, be sure that your child will be represented by someone who has his or her best interest at heart. Often the agent will opt to have a first meeting with the parent, and meet the child at the next meeting. Sometimes an agency will ask the parent to send in a snapshot and will notify the parent if the agency is interested.

Don't let the opinion of just one agency stop you from seeking out other agencies. And remember: Do not pay anyone any money for jobs, for auditions or for pictures

The most important person in this whole deal is your child. This is one time when the parents should really listen to their child.

CHAPTER XI

A Wrap? No! Just the Beginning!

Now that you've learned a little about the business of being in the movies as an extra–and if you're lucky as a principal–what do you think? Do you have what it takes to join the ranks of the unsung heroes of the industry?

Throughout this book you've read the facts as I and my fellow extras know them and live them. I've not white-washed my experiences nor have I made extras seem more put upon than we are. Before you start the process of breaking into the movies, you'd do well to ask yourself several questions:

- Is the pay less important to me than the process?
- Am I reliable? If I'm booked to be at a given place at a specific time, can I be depended upon to be there?
- Can I take direction–even by someone years my junior?
- Can I let those occasional sarcastic remarks not get to me?
- Do I have the physical stamina to work for hours in heat that would make Beelzebub feel at home or in cold that would make a polar bear shiver? Can I trudge up and down flights of stairs when it's part of the action?
- Can I get rejected time and time again without rejecting myself? This is a difficult one for most of us. I know how difficult from personal experience although I *have* had my share of victories. Some days it's the memory of those "yippee!" times that keeps me going back to try and try and try–even knowing that every now and then my spirit will feel as if it has gone though ten rounds with Mike Tyson. Just recently I was given a screen-test for a major motion

picture. I knew deep inside that I did a good, make that an excellent, job. Obviously the director who saw the film a day later didn't think I had the look that he wanted for that character. Wham! Maybe next time.

· Am I a team player? Can I get along with large numbers of people– often under less than ideal conditions?

· Do I understand that only a few people make a living acting in film? Does the catch phrase "Don't give up your day job" ring a bell? In case you think I'm joshing consider this: Bart Story Director of Research for the Screen Actors' Guild released this information (figures are from 1999–the most recent available as of this writing) Of the 98,000 SAG members 34,075 earned no money. That's right *no* money. Another 46,000 SAG members earned anywhere from $1.00-$5,000 (this is not a misprint). The remainder made over $5,000 (which is hardly enough for even a second-hand Bentley). Those SAG members who earned over $250,000 during 1999 were not included in these figures.

· Do I want to break into the movies with so much passion that I'm ready to "get going" *NOW*?

If you've answered "yes" to these questions, START NOW!

No one can register but *you*. No one can go to *your* auditions but *you*. Wanting to do it (regardless of what "it" is) never can take the place of actually doing it.

I wish I had ten dollars for every person with whom I've chatted at cocktail parties, counseled at my movie seminars, advised after lectures I've presented who gushed like Old Faithful about getting into this business and who, years later are still *gushing*, but not doing. If they have decided that the movie business isn't for them–fine, but I beg them: Stop bothering me unless you really are going to get off your collective duffs.

This lazy attitude reminds me of the fellow who read the lottery results week after week–and week after week was disappointed that he wasn't one of the winners. Finally, he cried up to the heavens, "Lord! Why can't I ever win?" "My son", came down the voice of God, "meet me halfway. BUY A TICKET!"

The ticket is, of course effort and commitment—regardless of what that sought after prize is. Not always, but more often than not, "I can't" actually means "I'm too lazy" or "I really don't want what I thought I wanted *enough* to put forth the effort".

Some people have told me that they're afraid of failing. Remember, it's far better to try something that you want to do and fail, than to do *nothing* and succeed.

I'll take you through the process stop-by-step.

Have a friend or relative take two colored snapshots of you. DO NOT SPEND MONEY ON EXPENSIVE PHOTOS. You won't be needing more than a snapshot until later, when you'll probably want to go after principal work—although many extras are satisfied with being extras and have no desire to do anything else.

Back to your picture. It should be in color. You should be dressed in upscale casual. One shot should be full length. Another shot should be closer (from just below the shoulders). Don't try for anything outrageous.

An aspiring actor (who either fancied himself a sexpot or thought that shock was his key to the door of opportunity) sent an agency for whom I was working, a full-length colored snapshot of himself standing on an apartment balcony. Had he not been standing there stark naked, he would have been a welcome addition to the files. What happened was that the photo was discarded—along with any chance that he'd be called by that agency.

- After you have your snapshots, call the agency with whom you'd like to register. There are several ways of getting connected with agents.
- *Look* in the Yellow Pages under Talent Agencies. Most libraries have phone directories from throughout the country.
- *Ask* those you know who are involved in *any* aspect of show business or entertainment for leads. Of course, if you know an honest-to-goodness extra, ask for help; extras are exceedingly generous when it comes to passing along information.
- *Research* the names, addresses, and phone numbers of hundreds of agencies listed on Business Discs available at most libraries. The research personnel at your library can be invaluable in helping to

find the agencies you'll need to get started. There's a disc specialized for casting directors and motion picture casting. These days libraries aren't only for checking out books. When you get the list of agencies call those in your area before you send anything out. Why? Because the disc is updated every two years, you want to be certain that the agency is still in business. While you're at it, check the address of the agency in question because if they've moved they try to keep the same phone number.

When you call ask how you can sign up, what they require, and if they do or do not allow "drop-ins". Some places have specific days and times that they'll see actors. Respect their rules.

Some of the agencies handle extras, some don't—they handle only principal work. As I mentioned earlier, being an extra is good—being a principal is "gooder". Starting as an extra is, however, a wise move.

· *Registering*: No matter which agency you contact, you'll need to submit a picture and fill out a registration card or an 8x10 sheet. Most places will ask you to send them a stamped, self-addressed envelope and then they'll send the registration material to you (unless they'd rather you come to the office). O.K., you've got the registration card—which has space for your photo. In addition to the space for name, address, phone number you'll be asked to include several other pieces of information. Think long and hard before you fill out the registration card. There's not much room, so you want to include all the best pieces of information about your accomplishments. Since that card will represent *you*, you'll want it to be as neat as possible.

Use a pen, print clearly. What to include: Besides your name, address, and phone numbers (include all numbers home, work, cell phone) fax, social security number. Generally, you'll be asked to list your car's color, year, make because, as I mentioned, if your car is used in a film you'll get extra money. List all your skills e.g.: dancing, swimming, languages other than English. If you play tennis, basketball, a musical instrument, etc, note it. Do you have formal wear, uniforms, business wear, wigs? Do you have a pet? Put that on your card too. You get the idea. Later in your career you'll need a résumé. I'll get to that later. Send your registration and snapshot to the agency. Sign with several agencies in order to have more chances of getting work. Be sure that when you *say* you have a skill that you really do have that skill. I got a nice silent bit in "Early Edition" because I could swim—not well, but I *could* swim. I told the director just that. It happened that the director bless him, wasn't looking for an Olympic grade aqua queen. Thank goodness I wasn't asked to *smoke* while I was swimming.

A director told me that he once selected an actor from half a dozen young men up for the part of a taxi driver. Comes the shoot date, the guy is seated behind the wheel of the cab and it turns out that the yahoo doesn't know how to drive!

After a few weeks you may want to give the agency a call to confirm that your card was indeed received. Make the inquiry polite, short and to the point.

You'd be wise to prepare yourself for the time when you're called to work.

Since you never know what season will be portrayed in any given movie, TV program, industrial, or educational film have a spring outfit ready in November, a winter coat, gloves, hat, boots for August. In other words, be prepared for any season at any time.

If you have an all-day exterior shoot in a part of the country that has a real honest-to-goodness winter season (snowing, blowing, hailing) be sure you have a selection of underwear and sweaters that can be layered, warm headgear and the warmest footwear you can find. You should know that warm feet on an extra during an exterior shoot with a wind chill factor of—20 degrees are as hard to find as caviar sandwiches in a school cafeteria.

· *Résumé*: Secure a résumé to the back of your 8x10 photo. Be sure that the résumé is cut to fit so that it doesn't extend beyond the picture. Some people staple the résumé to the picture. Not only does this look unattractive, but it looks even more tacky when you update your résumé and you must remove the four staples.

I use rubber cement on each of the four corners of my résumé to secure it because it looks better, and it's easy to remove without leaving tiny holes or tearing the picture. You'll be sending out a couple dozen headshots at a time. At about 40¢ a picture, it adds up.

 Don't include your phone number or your address. *Do* include your social security number. Why not include your phone number and address? Simple. Your picture, with résumé attached is sent by your agent, whose commission is 10%-15%, to a casting director and making independent deals with the actor is a no-no.

 Also, it's best to position your most impressive credits toward the top of your résumé because casting directors are busy people who don't (or won't) take the time to look at your entire résumé—so it makes sense to place your best work at the top . . . even if it's not chronologically accurate.

 At the beginning of your movie career you won't have many credits to list. So think very hard and list everything you've done in the area of show business. Make it as important as possible—without lying. For example, if you had the lead in "Auntie Mame" in high school or college, list it, but don't say when. If the casting person asks, tell the truth. Also, make a big deal out of your special abilities. This is the time to blow your own horn as if your name were Gabriel.

 So do you think that you're approaching the beginning of a new career? If the answer is yes, good luck, hang in there and keep your day job. Keep in mind that there are dozens of jobs other than acting in the movie industry: gaffer, grip, set designer, set dresser, painter, cameraman, caterer, assistant director, assistant *to* the director, wardrobe, makeup, hair, foley artist, stunt person, animal wrangler . . . the list goes on. There are scores of jobs which keep you right in the action but not acting.

 If you've got your heart set on acting in films, and you're willing to start out as an extra, I'll bet you're going to learn more than how movies are made.

 You're going to learn interesting things about yourself. Foremost, you may learn, as I did, that you're more independent than you thought. Having learned how to drive in the suburbs, my years behind the wheel took me within the borders of my small suburb. When I got into movies I not only had to drive into Chicago via the sociopath-infested expressway, but also to over-the-river-and-through-the-woods venues inaccessible via public transportation. The first few times were white-knuckle experiences, but I got used to it–and even managed to keep my palms reasonable dry during the trip. Like most things in life, if you want to do something you usually can overcome what you perceived to be an insurmountable obstacle.

It's also going to dawn on you that you're the kind of person who has inner strengths of which you weren't aware–this is true for both genders.

And because you'll meet all kinds of people, from all walks of life, you'll grow as a human being. You'll not be so quick to decide who you'd like to spend time talking with in the holding area or eating with at dinner time. Close friendships have developed between people who weren't that taken with each other when they were thrown together in a scene. Color, religion, social status, gender; none of these is as important as working together in a scene to satisfy the director.

When you become an extra you join the ranks of the unsung heroes of the industry who are so way down in the pecking order that they have no one to peck at, but still love what they do.

As I was writing this, the mail arrived. There's a request from a charity I think I've seen exposed on "Sixty Minutes", an offer to consolidate all my small bills into one humongous bill and an ad for novelty salt and pepper shakers. There was also an envelope from the Screen Actor's Guild. Inside is another gorgeous residual check. "Dennis the Menace" comes through again!

I love this business not only because of these checks which can brighten my day like rays of the sun brightening a dark room. I also love working in film because it's the kind of activity that keeps me feeling vibrant, and wondering what's next.

I see neighborhoods and people I'd probably never see–an education in itself.

Working in the movies has enhanced my enjoyment of viewing movies–even those I'm not in because I know a bit about what has gone into making even a less than monumental film.

With all the unknowns, with all the surprises, with all the ups and downs in the movie business one fact remains undisputed: You never know who's watching you and where or when your next break may come along. So whether you're a principal or an extra, whether you're placed in front of the camera, or so far from it that you'll need a taxi to get back to the holding area, do your best to get into the mood of the scene. I've seen extras who, as part of a crowd watching a horrendous accident, will stand there grinning and I've cringed when, during wedding scenes, I observed some of the background looking as if they were there to extend their sympathy to the relatives of the deceased. Get with the scene!

I once had a temp job working as an in-store demonstrator for a manufacturer of a top-of-the-line metal cream. Whenever anyone came anywhere near my display table I'd offer to polish a piece of jewelry for the individual. Because I usually sold out, the president of the company would mail me bonus checks. After a while, she came to see for herself where her money was going. Since we had never met face-to-face, I had no idea what she looked like. Apparently she liked the way I put my heart into so simple a thing as polishing someone's ring.

Long story short: Since that time I've accompanied her on many business trips throughout the United States and I've appeared over half a dozen times on TV's "Home Shopping Show". Recently I did a commercial for her product.

And it all started with polishing a ring. So whenever you're in a scene, give it your best. Shine!

Who's Who and What's What

Some terms you'll hear in the business

AFTRA: American Federation of Radio and Television Artists. This union works to secure the optimum working conditions and pay for those in radio and television. There's a pretty hefty membership fee, as well as twice yearly dues (the latter dependent upon how much you earn). To work in union productions, membership is mandatory. Under the Taft-Hartley Law an actor may work in his first union project without being a union member—and, further, may work in as many union projects within 30 days as he wishes without his having to join the union. After 30 days he *must* join if he wishes to work in a union project.

Agent: The individual who represents the actor by submitting the talent's picture and résumé to the casting director or client. The agent receives a commission of anywhere from 10% to 20% of the fee that's earned.

Back to one: Go back to the spot you were first placed. Also known as "re-set".

Booking: A job. When your agent says "I have a booking for you", it's like a love song.

Buyout: A lump sum of money offered by a client (the "customer", the final word on which actor gets the job aka the booking and what the fee will be). The buyout is in place of residuals. I once agreed to accept a buyout, and, as it turned out, the commercial ran for 3½ years throughout the United States–including Alaska and Hawaii. Why did I accept an $850 buyout? If I refused that deal I probably wouldn't have gotten the booking. I have no delusions of grandeur. There are hundreds, perhaps thousands of actors in my city alone who would have accepted that deal.

I don't think that I'm God's gift to show business. Yes, I did a job on that commercial that I was pleased with–and so was the client. Who knew it would run for 3½ years? I'm the kind of person who belongs to the "bird in the hand" school of thought–even thought a bird in the hand *can* get a bit messy.

Call Time: The time you're instructed to check in for a shoot. Arrive fifteen minutes before that time. Tip: If you know that there will be many extras you'd be wise to arrive even earlier so that you can get a decent parking spot.

Casting Director: The individual who works with the director to find the most appropriate actor for a given project. The casting director gets submissions from the agent via pictures, résumés and/or video tapes.

Cattlecall: A notice, usually in newspapers or on the radio inviting actors–and, often, the general public to assemble at a given location so that the casting director can see a huge number of people (therefore "cattlecall") for possible work in an upcoming project. Your agent isn't involved at that point. Take along a headshot, if you have one, and/or a color snapshot. At most catllecalls a Polaroid will be taken of you. Try to get to the call very early or toward the end of the designated time frame when there is the chance of a smaller crowd. Take something to do while you're in line.

Continuity: The process which assures that actions and objects stay the same from one take to the next. Example: If a woman is holding a handbag in her right hand and a newspaper in her left during the first take, that's exactly what she must be holding in the proper hands during the next take and the ones after that–for as long as it "takes" for the director to be satisfied. The "same" rule applies to where and how the props are positioned. Everything must match.

Copy: The script that is used for a commercial or other television work. In TV and movie work the copy is referred to as "sides".

Cut!: Means that the director wants the cameras to stop–and of course– for the action to stop.

Director: Main Man, Top Dog, Highest Honcho, Numero Uno, Four-Star General, Rear-Admiral, Commander-in-Chief. You get the idea. You do not talk to him (unless he speaks to you first). You don't give him your picture and résumé. You don't give him a script for a film that is destined to win every Oscar in the book. In other words: DO NOT BOTHER THE DIRECTOR.

A year or so before I got into this business I was walking through Central Park in Manhattan where a scene for "Tootsie" was being filmed. I walked over to the director Sydney Pollack, and struck up a conversation with him about one of my daughters who was studying film in college. We spoke for a few minutes during which he was charming.

I wouldn't *think* of doing anything like that now.

Freeze: Don't move! If you're in the middle of a take and you hear "freeze" do just that. There are several reasons for this command. Just do it.

Iced: When a client or casting director selects an actor for a project, but said client doesn't have a definite date in mind, the actor is asked to reserve one or two dates designated by the client—although neither of the dates is an actual booking—yet. These dates are "iced". Why is the term called "iced"? I think it's because those dates are frozen in time—and the actor is waiting for the thaw!

Industrial: A film that's used to instruct employees of a business or corporation. Educational films are used to instruct in a scholastic or professional area.

I-9: A document you must fill out to indicate that you're eligible to be employed in the United States. Bring two pieces of identification with you to the location.

Lock it up: Stopping pedestrian and/or street traffic for a short time while a scene is being shot. Most citizens are good sports about this—but a few get hot under the collar about the delay.

Look-see: Like an audition, but usually without lines. As the term implies, the client is looking for a certain type (who may or may not get lines in the production). Bring your headshot and résumé, but a Polaroid will be taken at the look-see. The "look" is the primary concern.

Lose It: When I was told, for the first time, "Lose your hat, Leona", I didn't know that what was meant was "Don't wear your hat in this scene". Since then I've been asked to "lose" my glasses, a too bright coat or a scarf.

Mark: The place where the actor is instructed to stand. An actual mark is placed on the floor which enables the camera and the sound to be adjusted for various angles and distances within a given scene.

New Deal: Has nothing to do with FDR. The call "new deal!" means that the scene you've just been working in finished and that a new scene is going to be set up. You'll either be instructed to stay close or go back to the holding area to wait for a call to the "New Deal".

O.T.: Overtime. If you're getting $55 for eight hour's work and you have a one hour dinner or lunch break, after nine hours you'll start getting paid time and a half for each hour after that.

Political: An individual usually an extra without an agent who is working on a shoot thanks to the fact that he or she knows a big wig (or a medium wig) in the production company. Often these people are placed in prime spots in the shoot.

Print work: Photo work for catalogues, newspaper adds, brochures. Pay is excellent, working conditions good, hours short. If you want to get into this aspect of the business, have composites made: several poses showing you in various outfits and "characters". Good choices are business, parent, sport, teacher, etc. . . . depending upon you age and "look" (there's that word again!)

Residuals: Monies received, aside from actual pay for a given project for future uses of a movie or filmed commercial.

I receive about three or four checks a year from any sales of "Dennis the Menace", showings on TV and rentals. Of course, my share is tiny, but none-the-less much welcomed.

Rolling!: When this call is shouted on the set be quiet. Be very quiet. It means that the sound is rolling and every little whisper and movement can be picked up by the sensitive equipment.

SAG: Screen Actors Guild: Same purpose as AFTRA but for those working in the film industry.

Storyboard: Before going into the studio for a TV edition, you'll often be told to study the storyboard which is a series of sketches of the action as it will be filmed segment by segment.

Stand-in: An individual who takes the place of a principal primarily so that adjusting the camera angles and color adjustment can be made without bothering the star. After the technical work is completed, the principal steps in for the actual shooting of the scene.

I've been a stand-in a few times. The pay scale is a bit higher than extra work. It's interesting to be close to the action and ready to step into the scene. Once-in-a-while the stand-in and the star become friends. And, oh yes—you can take stuff from the craft table (how lucky can you get!)

The stand-in should match the principal as closely as possible in height, weight and coloring.

Upgrade: Getting additional money for doing something more than background work—such as that hip action I did in "Vice-Versa". My interaction with Ness in "The Untouchables" should have garnered me an upgrade, but the production company didn't do what they should have done, but sometimes it pays to fuhgedaboudit.

V/O: Voice-over. Only the voice of the actor is heard on a TV commercial over the picture. Excellent pay. Lots of competition. No wardrobe to pack and pull. Fast and fun.

Work Permit: Required for all children up to age sixteen. The permit is obtained through the child's school. A doctor's statement is also required, as well. Best to check with the labor department in the state in which you reside.

Wrap: It's a wrap! Means filming is done for the day–and as tired as you are, as happy as you are that you're on your way home after a 12, 14, or 15 hour day, you're hoping it won't be too long before you get another booking.

On days when things aren't going "thumbs up" in my career. I take comfort in this bit of philosophy penned by Anonymous (she's written so many inspiring words).

I have fought many a battle and lost, but I have won enough battles to make me believe in the struggle and keep on fighting.

I have trusted may a person who railed me, but I have found enough true friends to make me forever believe in humanity and keep on trusting.

I have dreamed many a dream that never came true, but I have had enough dreams come true to make me forever believe in dreams and keep on dreaming.

From one of my actor friends, Jon Bellezza aka Jonny Bell:

> Life is like a movie.
> Life is like a movie and you're the actor.
> You're the director and you're the writer.
> If you do not like the way your life is going,
> You'd better change the script, because it's your life-
> And you have a lot to say about how it goes.
> *You* have the power to be the "star" of your life!

And from me–

May all your movies have happy endings–especially your documentaries.

The following was sent to me; I don't know who wrote it. As a frequent movie-goer I got a kick out of these film fun facts which have nothing to do with the subject of this book, but there's always room for a laugh.

Things You Would Never Know If It Weren't For The Movies

· Large, loft apartments in New York City are plentiful and affordable, even if the tenants are unemployed.

· One of a pair of identical twins is evil.

· Should you decide to defuse a bomb, don't worry about which wire to cut. You will always choose the right one.

· It doesn't matter if you are greatly outnumbered in a fight involving marital arts. Your enemies will wait patiently to attack you one by one dancing around in a threatening manner until you have dispatched their predecessors.

· When you turn out the light to go to bed, everything in your bedroom will still be clearly visible but slightly blue.

· If you are blonde and pretty, it is possible to be a world-famous expert on nuclear fission, dinosaurs, hieroglyphics, or anything else, at the age of 22.

· Honest and hard-working policemen are usually gunned down a day or two before retirement.

· Rather than wasting bullets, megalomaniacs prefer to kill their enemies using complex machinery involving fuses, deadly gasses, lasers, buzz saws and hungry sharks, all of which will give their captives at least 20 minutes to escape.

· During all crime investigations, it is necessary to visit a strip club at least once.

· All beds have special L-shaped covers that reach up to the armpits of a woman but only to the waist of the man lying beside her.

· All grocery shopping bags contain at least one French bread and one bunch of carrots with leafy tops.

· It's easy to land a plane, providing there is someone in the control tower to talk you down.

- If you are beautiful, your makeup never rubs off, even while scuba-diving or fighting aliens. However if you are overweight your mascara will run and your lipstick will smear.
- The ventilation system of any building is the perfect hiding place. No one will ever think of looking for you in there, and you can travel to any other part of the building without difficulty.
- You're very likely to survive any battle in any war unless you make the mistake of showing someone a picture of your sweetheart back home.
- Should you wish to pass yourself off as a German officer, it is not necessary to speak the language. A German accent will do.
- A man will show no pain while taking the most horrific beating, but will wince when a woman tries to clean his wounds.
- If staying in a haunted house, women must investigate any strange noises in their most diaphanous underwear, which is what they happened to be wearing when the car broke down.
- If someone says "I'll be right back", they won't.
- Even when driving down a perfectly straight road, it is necessary to turn the steering wheel from time to time.
- All bombs are fitted with electronic timing devices with large red readouts so you know exactly when they're going to go off.
- A police detective can only solve a case after he has been suspended from duty.
- If you decide to start dancing in the street, everyone around you will be able to mirror all the steps you come up with, and hear the music in your head.
- Police departments give their officers personality tests to make sure each is assigned a partner who is their total opposite.
- When they are alone, all foreigners prefer to speak English to each other.

Keep your sense of humor (you'll need it), good luck and here's to a lot of camera time!

Names • Addresses • Notes

Names • Addresses • Notes

Names • *Addresses* • *Notes*

Names • Addresses • Notes

Names • Addresses • Notes